TITLES IN THIS
EDITED AND INTRODUCED BY M

Cuba and Angola: Fighting for Africa's Freedom and Our Own
by Fidel Castro, Raúl Castro, Nelson Mandela, and others (2013)

Women and Revolution: The Living Example of the Cuban Revolution
by Asela de los Santos and Mary-Alice Waters (2013)

Women in Cuba: The Making of a Revolution Within the Revolution
by Vilma Espín, Asela de los Santos, and Yolanda Ferrer (2012)

The Cuban Five
by Martín Koppel and Mary-Alice Waters (2012)

Soldier of the Cuban Revolution
by Luis Alfonso Zayas (2011)

Capitalism and the Transformation of Africa
by Mary-Alice Waters and Martín Koppel (2009)

The First and Second Declarations of Havana
(2007)

Our History Is Still Being Written
by Armando Choy, Gustavo Chui, and Moisés Sío Wong (2005)

Aldabonazo
by Armando Hart (2004)

Marianas in Combat
by Teté Puebla (2003)

October 1962: The 'Missile' Crisis as Seen from Cuba
by Tomás Diez Acosta (2002)

From the Escambray to the Congo
by Víctor Dreke (2002)

Playa Girón/Bay of Pigs
by Fidel Castro and José Ramón Fernández (2001)

Cuba and the Coming American Revolution
by Jack Barnes (2001)

Fertile Ground: Che Guevara and Bolivia
by Rodolfo Saldaña (2001)

(continued on next page)

Che Guevara Talks to Young People
(2000)

Making History
Interviews with four Cuban generals (1999)

Pombo: A Man of Che's *guerrilla*
by Harry Villegas (1997)

At the Side of Che Guevara
by Harry Villegas (1997)

Episodes of the Cuban Revolutionary War, 1956–58
by Ernesto Che Guevara (1996)

The Bolivian Diary of Ernesto Che Guevara
(1994)

To Speak the Truth
by Fidel Castro and Ernesto Che Guevara (1992)

How Far We Slaves Have Come!
by Nelson Mandela and Fidel Castro (1991)

U.S. Hands Off the Mideast!
by Fidel Castro and Ricardo Alarcón (1990)

In Defense of Socialism
by Fidel Castro (1989)

Che Guevara: Economics and Politics in the Transition to Socialism
by Carlos Tablada (1989)

CUBA AND ANGOLA

Cuba & Angola
Fighting for Africa's Freedom and Our Own

FIDEL CASTRO

RAÚL CASTRO

NELSON MANDELA

The CUBAN FIVE in Angola:
In their own words

Including accounts by four generals of Cuba's Revolutionary Armed Forces

Armando Choy ∞ **Gustavo Chui**
Moisés Sío Wong ∞ **Luis Alfonso Zayas**

and

Gabriel García Márquez *on* Operation Carlota

PATHFINDER
New York London Montreal Sydney

Edited by Mary-Alice Waters
Copyright © 2013 by Pathfinder Press
All rights reserved

ISBN 978-1-60488-046-5
Library of Congress Control Number 2012956385
Manufactured in the United States of America

Cover design: Toni Gorton
Cover photos: Clockwise from center, Cuban and Angolan combatants with South African tank captured in battle, Cuito Cuanavale, 1988 • Independence day, Luanda, Angola, November 11, 1975 • Nelson Mandela and Fidel Castro, July 26, 1991, Matanzas, Cuba • Gerardo Hernández, one of Cuban Five in US prisons, (rear, right), with Cuban and Angolan combatants from his reconnaissance unit, during internationalist mission in Angola, 1989–90 • Angolan students with Cuban instructor at Luanda Hospital nursing school, 1976 • One of Cuban ground crews responsible for maintaining MiG fighters that drove South African planes out of southern Angola skies, 1988.

Pathfinder
www.pathfinderpress.com
E-mail: pathfinder@pathfinderpress.com

Contents

Introduction 9
Mary-Alice Waters

The Cuban internationalist mission in Angola 15

I. Defending Angola's independence and sovereignty

Consolidating a powerful bulwark
against apartheid South Africa 21
Fidel Castro (September 1975)

African blood flows through our veins 31
Fidel Castro (December 1975)

Angola: An African Girón 35
Fidel Castro (April 1976)

We staked everything in Angola 41
Fidel Castro (December 1988)

All we take with us from Africa are the remains
of our combatants who died fighting for freedom 51
Fidel Castro (December 1989)

Thanks to Angola, we know better
what we are capable of achieving 59
Raúl Castro (May 1991)

II. An unparalleled contribution to African freedom

The crushing defeat of the racist army at Cuito Cuanavale
was a victory for the whole of Africa 73
Nelson Mandela (July 1991)

The most profound tribute ever paid
to our internationalist fighters 77
Fidel Castro (July 1991)

III. The Cuban Revolution was strengthened

The people of Cuba were behind our effort 81
Armando Choy, Gustavo Chui, and Moisés Sío Wong (2005)

Our volunteers learned what Cuba used to be like 93
Luis Alfonso Zayas (2011)

IV. The Cuban Five in Angola—In their own words

Gerardo Hernández: Angola was a school for everyone 107
Mary-Alice Waters (August 2010)

Twelve men and two cats: With Gerardo Hernández and his platoon in Angola 109
Zenia Regalado with José Luis Palacio (March 2006)

I learned more than from all the books I studied or could have studied 113
Fernando González (December 2012)

Angola taught me that the most beautiful works are accomplished by imperfect men 117
René González (June 2005)

V. Operation Carlota

Operation Carlota 123
Gabriel García Márquez (1977)

Glossary of individuals, organizations, and events 137

Introduction

Mary-Alice Waters

Cuban internationalists have made a contribution to African independence, freedom, and justice, unparalleled for its principled and selfless character.
NELSON MANDELA
Matanzas, Cuba, July 1991

When we face new and unexpected challenges we will always be able to recall the epic of Angola with gratitude, because without Angola we would not be as strong as we are today.
RAÚL CASTRO
Havana, Cuba, May 1991

Between 1975 and 1991, some 425,000 Cubans volunteered for duty in Angola in response to requests from the government of that country, which had just wrested freedom from Portugal after nearly five centuries of brutal exploitation and colonial domination. The mission: helping to defend Angola against what stretched into thirteen years of military aggression, including two major invasions, by the armed forces of the apartheid regime of South Africa and its African and imperialist allies.

The stakes were enormous.

In April 1974 the fifty-year-old, deeply decayed fascist dictatorship in Portugal was overthrown by a military coup that unleashed a powerful revolutionary upsurge of Portuguese workers and farmers. The confidence of Europe's capitalist rulers was shaken.

In April 1975 US imperialism was literally driven out of Indochina. The whole world watched—in joy or horror, depending on your class perspective—as helicopters scrambled to rescue thousands of desperate American officials and their Vietnamese lackeys from the rooftop of Washington's embassy in what had just become Ho Chi Minh City.

Anti-imperialist struggles of a more and more popular character were deepening in Iran, Grenada, Nicaragua, and elsewhere in Central America.

Not losing control of southern Africa was rising in the priorities of the imperialist powers. For years they had been maneuvering to salvage what they could as the Portuguese empire crumbled. With Angolan independence day approaching in November 1975, they accelerated their efforts to install what they hoped would be a compliant puppet regime in the largest and richest of Portugal's former African territories. For Pretoria—backhandedly encouraged and supplied by Washington—the future of all southern Africa, including the survival of the apartheid regime itself, was on the table.

The first major invasion of Angola by South African troops began in October 1975 as armored columns crossed the border from their de facto colony of South-West Africa (Namibia) and swept north. Simultaneously a military offensive moved south from Zaire (Congo). The pro-imperialist Mobutu dictatorship there hoped to annex the oil-rich Angolan province of Cabinda and take whatever other territory they could. The objective was to conquer Luanda, the capital city, before November 11 to prevent the installation of a government headed by the Popular Movement for the Liberation of Angola (MPLA), the strongest of the independence movements, with the broadest popular base.

It was only the eleventh-hour intervention of some six hundred fifty Cuban internationalist volunteers, responding to the urgent request of Angola's provisional government for aid, that prevented the South African objectives from being realized. Less than five months later, with thirty-six thousand Cuban volunteers by then on the ground, the military forces of both the South African apartheid regime and the Zairean dictatorship had been driven out of Angola. But they had not given up.

More than a decade of what was euphemistically known as "low intensity warfare" against the Angolan regime ensued. Then, in late 1987, South African troops began their second major invasion, which ended with the crushing defeat of Pretoria's military forces in March 1988 in the now-famous battle of Cuito Cuanavale.

As South African anti-apartheid struggle leader Nelson Mandela told the world three years later, "Cuito Cuanavale was a milestone in the history of the struggle for southern African liberation! . . . A turning point in the struggle to free the continent and our country from the scourge of apartheid!"

That decisive victory not only secured the sovereignty of Angola. It also allowed the people of Namibia to achieve their independence from South African apartheid rule and gave a powerful boost to the rising mass revolutionary struggle against white supremacist rule in South Africa itself. Less than two years after the victory at Cuito Cuanavale, Nelson Mandela, imprisoned for more than twenty-seven years, was free. Four years later the apartheid regime was no more, and Nelson Mandela was president of South Africa.

In the pages that follow, this history is told by those who lived it and made it.

❧

The contribution made by hundreds of thousands of Cuban internationalists, military and civilian alike, to the independence struggles in southern Africa was not a "favor" to others, however. The Cuban Revolution, the strength of its proletarian core, was also at stake. As Minister of the Revolutionary Armed Forces Raúl Castro told the Cuban people in May 1991 as he welcomed home the last contingent of volunteers, "If our people know themselves better, if all of us know much better what we are capable of achieving—veterans as well as our young people, the new generations—that, too, is thanks to Angola!"

Among the "new generations" whose lives were transformed as they fought side by side with the people of Angola were three young Cubans, still in their twenties, whose names are today known around the world: Gerardo Hernández, Fernando González, and René González. They are three of the five Cubans who, a few years after their experiences in Angola, volunteered for another internationalist assignment, this time in the United States. Their mission: monitoring the activities of Cuban American counterrevolutionary organizations operating with impunity from bases in the US, groups that organize to carry out violent actions against supporters of the revolution inside Cuba, the US, Puerto Rico, and elsewhere, and whose actions always contain a threat of precipitating a confrontation between Washington and Cuba. Arrested by the FBI in 1998, and framed up on more than thirty charges, the Cuban Five have been imprisoned in the US for more than fourteen years.

As Fernando González writes in the account published in these pages, the lessons he learned in Angola are ones he has continued to draw on ever since, "including here, withstanding conditions of prolonged imprisonment."

❧

The final and decisive battles waged in 1988 in Angola by more than fifty thousand Cuban volunteers coincided with, and in turn advanced, what was known in Cuba as the rectification process, one of the most important chapters in the history of the revolution.

In April 1986, speaking on the occasion of the twenty-fifth anniversary of the victory at Playa Girón that crushed the US-organized invasion of Cuba at the Bay of Pigs, Cuban president Fidel Castro announced the leadership's decision to initiate a profound correction in the course of the revolution. He likened it to a ship altering its compass headings in order to sail on a different path. For more than a decade, as policies associated with an Economic Planning and Management System copied from the Soviet Union had been introduced, proletarian initiatives and collective efforts by Cuba's workers and small farmers had become progressively weaker.

Fidel summed up the error with great insight many years later in November 2005 when he told an audience of young leaders of the revolution that "among the many errors we all have committed, the most important was to believe that someone knew something about socialism, or knew how to build socialism. As if it were an exact science, as well known as an electrical system conceived by those who considered themselves experts in electrical systems. When they said, 'Here is the formula,' we thought they knew."

As the rectification process unfolded, encouraging the creativity and imagination of Cuba's toilers again became the driving force of the revolution, combating the economic, social, and political weight of what had become an increasingly bloated, and relatively privileged, administrative layer in the mills, factories, ministries, offices, and mass organizations.

Wages for agricultural workers, among the lowest paid in the country, were raised by 40 percent. Special clinics, stores, restaurants, and recreational facilities established by the Ministry of the Interior for its personnel were turned over to general use by the population. Privileged access to state cars, gas rations, and special entertainment budgets were curtailed.

Volunteer full-time minibrigades involving tens of thousands of workers were established in workplaces across the country mobilizing almost overnight a workforce eager to help accomplish the most urgently needed social priorities—housing, child care centers, clinics, schools, recreational facilities, and more. Larger volunteer construction contingents—in which wages, hours, and work rules were decided and implemented by the workers themselves—took on the building of roads, dams, hospitals, airports, and other major infrastructure projects.

Volunteer labor—the centerpiece of proletarian action in the early years of the revolution, which "took refuge in defense activities" during what Fidel in 1987 called that "shameful period in the building of socialism"—was reborn "like a phoenix." As the minibrigades took on the character of a mass social movement, "The bureaucrat's view, the technocrat's view that voluntary work was neither basic nor essential" lost ground.

This was the revolutionary course advancing in Cuba as the final great battles of the Angola war were joined. It was the spirit that marked the forty thousand Cuban volunteers on the Southern Front in Angola who together with their Angolan and Namibian comrades-in-arms fought their way east and south in the opening months of 1988, building a forward airfield in seventy days as they raised the siege at Cuito Cuanavale, cleared minefields and roads, and took control of the air.

It was all over. The apartheid regime was forced to withdraw from Namibia as well as Angola and sue for peace.

※

The victory represented by Cuito Cuanavale, together with the deepening proletarian course in Cuba itself, also allowed the revolution to confront and emerge strengthened from one of the bitterest moments it had faced in thirty years.

In June and July 1989, evidence was uncovered by the military high command that Division General Arnaldo Ochoa, Hero of the Republic of Cuba, who headed the Angolan mission in 1987–88, had been supervising sugar sales on the black market in Angola as well as amateur trafficking in diamonds and ivory as the lives of thousands of Cuban and Angolan combatants hung in the balance at Cuito Cuanavale.

As Fidel expressed it with unflinching clarity, "At the same time that the most glorious page was being written, the most shameful one was being written, in large measure by the head of the Cuban military mission in Angola."

The *Granma* editorial announcing Ochoa's arrest pointedly made clear, however, that it was Division General Leopoldo Cintra Frías, not Ochoa, who had been given command of the Southern Front "to ensure the complete success of our troops' operations in Angola." That was where "the bulk of the Cuban personnel, tanks, artillery, antiaircraft forces, and air force units were stationed." Ochoa, the editorial noted, was "involved in other tasks for the Cuban military mission," tasks that were removed from "the course of military events."

As a widening investigation by the Cuban government soon revealed, the small-scale illegal operations in Angola were the least of Ochoa's offenses. He had also been supervising the activities of one of his aides, whom Ochoa had authorized to meet with Pablo Escobar of the Medellín drug cartel and other narcotics dealers to explore options for trafficking operations using Cuban air and sea lanes and possible cocaine laboratories in Africa. The motivation, Ochoa claimed, was a desire to raise money—big money, $4 billion was the sum he used—to buy military equipment for Angola and Cuba and speed development of a tourist industry in Cuba.

Ochoa and his subordinate were court-martialed and executed, together with two high-ranking officers of the Ministry of the Interior who, the investigation revealed, had already been engaged in their own drug-trafficking operations, in addition to facilitating Ochoa's schemes.

It was a traumatic moment in Cuba.

Division General Enrique Carreras gave eloquent voice to the popular outrage a few years later when he commented in an interview, "Imagine sullying our uniform for money, to get out of an economic bind! That's what Ochoa did. And this in an army as honorable as the Rebel Army! If we have to die of hunger we'll die of hunger, but we won't disgrace what the people have fought for so hard and so long. We won't disgrace what so many people have died for over the years. . . . That's why we fought for socialism—to eliminate such evils."

Extensive excerpts of the proceedings of the Military Court of Honor, the court martial testimony, and the review of the death sentences by the Council of State were published in the daily paper *Granma*, broadcast on TV and radio, and followed closely by millions of Cubans. By the end of what became known in Cuba as Case No. 1 in 1989, there was broad, though far from unanimous, agreement among Cuban working people with the justice of the sentences—and their necessity.

"Who would ever believe in the revolution again," Fidel asked, "if we did not actually apply the most severe sentences established by our legislation for crimes of this gravity?"

"Who would ever speak of rectification again?"

A July 9 meeting of the Council of State reviewed and then ratified the sentences for Ochoa and the other three. At the conclusion of his remarks, Raúl Castro reminded everyone that as the commander of the military mission in Angola, Ochoa had signed death sentences for three young Cuban soldiers who had been convicted of rape and murder of Angolan women. As minister of the Revolutionary Armed Forces, Raúl had been responsible for ratifying those orders, which he had done.

"I didn't hesitate," Raúl said, "because the decision was just. Nor will I hesitate when I sign the sentence requested by the court in these four cases considered by the Council of State. The mothers of those three young men might have asked for clemency. If we don't carry out this sentence, we will have to beg them for forgiveness."

❧

By the time the last units of internationalist volunteers returned from Angola in 1991, Cuba was already confronting the greatest political and economic crisis in its history. With the implosion of the bureaucratized regime in the Soviet Union came an abrupt loss of 85 percent of Cuba's foreign trade. As virtually all imports evaporated, agricultural and industrial production collapsed. It was "as if one day the sun didn't rise," Fidel said.

As the crisis deepened, Cuba's enemies, blindly convinced of their own myths of dwindling support for the revolution, were once again predicting (hoping for) its imminent demise. And in fact, no other government in the world could have survived such a crisis. But Cuba had never been a tropical version of what the Soviet Union had become, or the countries of Eastern Europe had always been. In class terms, it was their political and moral negation. And the confidence of Cuba's toilers in themselves and their government, "in what we are capable of achieving," to use Raúl's words, was in no small measure due to the conquests registered in the Angolan internationalist mission and the rectification process.

The fifty thousand Cubans who volunteered for duty in Angola in 1988 to assure the crushing defeat of the apartheid army in the battle of Cuito Cuanavale would have been equivalent at the time, in population terms, to the United States fielding 1.2 million troops in a theater of operations. That's just one measure of the enormity of the internationalist commitment made by the men and women of the Cuban Revolution. Yet to new generations of revolutionists and militant, thinking working people around the world, all this is virtually a hidden history.

A handful of memoirs have been published in Cuba by those who fought on one or another front during the nearly sixteen-year mission. Virtually none have been translated or published outside Cuba. Moreover, no comprehensive account yet exists, although this may change with the scheduled publication in September 2013 of *Visions of Freedom:*

Havana, Washington, and Pretoria in Southern Africa, 1976–1991 by Piero Gleijeses, author of the excellent study *Conflicting Missions: Havana, Washington, and Africa, 1959–76*, which covers the opening months of the mission.

Cuba and Angola: Fighting for Africa's Freedom and Our Own aims to make a small contribution to filling the void and encouraging those who took part in what Fidel called "Cuba's greatest internationalist feat ever" to make that history known.

Readers will find its strength in the multiple perspectives it offers on many of the same events.

Through the speeches of Fidel Castro, commander in chief of the Angola internationalist mission and historic leader of the Cuban Revolution, and those of Raúl Castro, then minister of the Revolutionary Armed Forces of Cuba, we are given the broadest political, strategic, and military view. Why the Cuban leadership took the decisions it did at important junctures. How these decisions were implemented and led. And the consequences for the revolution and its relations with other world powers and national liberation forces in Africa, Latin America, and elsewhere.

Nelson Mandela, the historic leader of the struggle to rid his country, his continent, and the world of the scourge of apartheid, explains the unprecedented political character of Cuba's actions in Africa, their weight and place in world history.

Armando Choy, Gustavo Chui, Moisés Sío Wong, and Alfonso Zayas, four historic combatants of the struggle to overthrow the Batista dictatorship, give us the perspective of four generals of the Revolutionary Armed Forces of Cuba. Each of them was among the seasoned frontline officers, leading in different capacities on the battlefields of Angola and in Cuba.

Through the accounts of Gerardo Hernández, Fernando González, and René González, we see the Angolan internationalist mission as it was lived by the then youngest generations of revolutionaries —how they were molded by that combat experience and transformed for life.

And in Gabriel García Márquez's "Operation Carlota," one of the greatest contemporary Latin American authors documents the opening of the Angola campaign and its first great victories. Through his eyes we see the impact that those events had on the fighting determination of Cuban working people—from the new beats in their music to the added bounce in their steps and broader smiles on their faces.

Cuba and Angola: Fighting for Africa's Freedom and Our Own is dedicated to the men and women of Cuba who wrote this epic chapter in the history of their revolution—and to those then too young to have participated, who will learn from it and from each other as they march into the class battles whose initial flares are already burning.

JANUARY 2013

THE CUBAN INTERNATIONALIST MISSION IN ANGOLA

Between November 1975 and May 1991, more than 375,000 members of Cuba's Revolutionary Armed Forces volunteered to serve in Angola in response to requests from the government of that newly independent country for help in turning back two major invasions and ongoing military operations by South Africa's apartheid regime. An additional 50,000 internationalist volunteers carried out various civilian responsibilities. The thirteen-year campaign by imperialism's South African junior partner to overthrow the Angolan government was carried out in alliance with counterrevolutionary Angolan forces that received substantial US financial, military, and diplomatic support.

In the end, however, the apartheid regime and its allies and backers were defeated.

Cuba's active support to the independence struggle in Africa's Portuguese colonies had begun more than a decade before Angola won its independence. In the opening months of 1965 Ernesto Che Guevara visited Africa and met with leaders of national liberation struggles in Angola, Mozambique, Guinea-Bissau, and Cape Verde, pledging Cuba's full support to their struggle to overturn Lisbon's colonial rule. A few months later Guevara himself led a six-month mission of 128 Cuban combatants to the former Belgian colony of the Congo to assist anti-imperialist forces there.

Over the next ten years, Cuban internationalists aided the movements in Portugal's African colonies. In 1974 the Portuguese dictatorship, which had come to power in the late 1920s, was brought down by a military coup. The fall of the dictatorship unleashed a massive revolutionary upsurge of working people and youth, accelerated by the impact of the spreading armed liberation struggles in Africa. Portugal's colonies gained their independence.

Angola was to become independent on November 11, 1975, with a government led by the MPLA (Popular Movement for the Liberation of Angola), the strongest liberation movement in the country. In an attempt to block that from happening, the army of the South African apartheid regime invaded Angola, coming across Angola's southern border shared with Namibia, which was then under South African rule. An anticolonial struggle was under way in Namibia as well, led by the South West Africa People's Organisation (SWAPO).

The South African invasion of Angola was backed by Washington and aided by the proimperialist government of Zaire (the former Belgian Congo). Among other goals, Zaire's President Mobutu Sese Seko hoped to annex Angola's oil-rich Cabinda province.

The objective of the South African and US rulers was to stop the MPLA from forming the new government and instead hand over power to Pretoria and Washington's allies in UNITA (National Union for the Total Independence of Angola), led by Jonas Savimbi, and the FNLA (National Front for the Liberation of Angola), led by Holden Roberto. By early November, the South African forces and their allies were closing in on Angola's capital city of Luanda.

Angola's new president, Agostinho Neto, appealed to the Cuban government for combat forces to help prevent the South African forces from taking Luanda. Cuba's internationalist response was recounted by Colombian author Gabriel García Márquez following extensive interviews with Cuban leaders. "The leadership of the Communist Party of Cuba had no more than twenty-four hours to make the decision," he wrote in 1977, "which it did, without vacillation, on November 5. . . . The

Angola

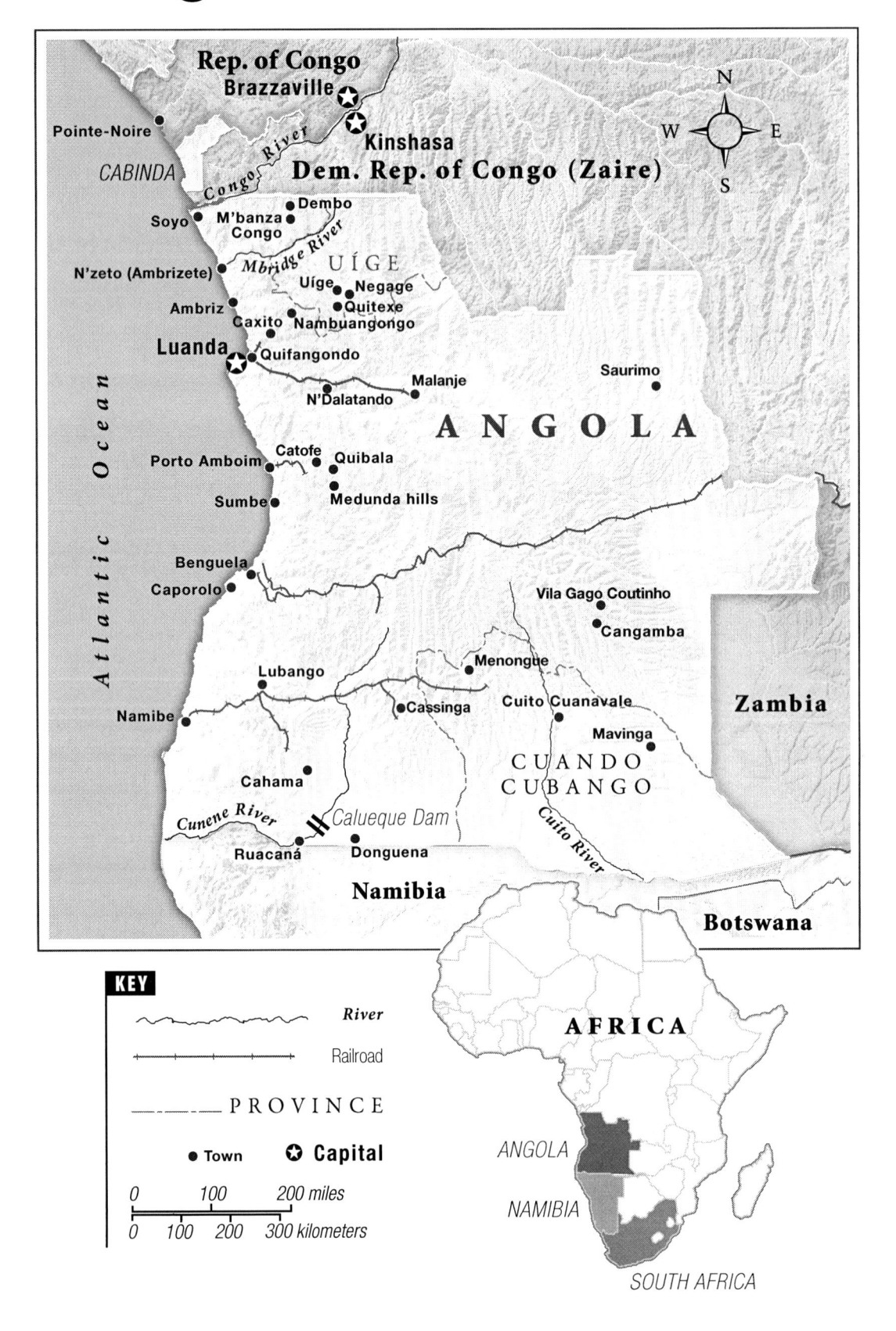

decision was an independent and sovereign act of Cuba. It was only after it was made, not before, that Cuba notified the Soviet Union."[1]

The mission was named Operation Carlota, after a slave woman from the Triunvirato sugar mill near Matanzas, Cuba, known as "Black Carlota." Armed with a machete, she led a slave rebellion in 1843 that extended to a number of plantations in the province. She was captured and drawn and quartered by the Spanish colonial troops.

The Cuban internationalists were decisive in halting the invading forces a few kilometers outside Luanda, a matter of hours before the independence ceremony. They then helped lead a counteroffensive both to the north and to the south. By March 27, 1976, "when the last South African soldiers crossed the Namibian border after a retreat of more than seven hundred kilometers, one of the most brilliant pages in the liberation of black Africa had been written," said Fidel Castro on April 19, 1976.[2]

Tens of thousands in Cuba had volunteered to be part of the effort. "The immense majority went to Angola with the full conviction that they were carrying out an act of political solidarity. They went with the same consciousness and courage they had displayed fifteen years earlier when they defeated the Bay of Pigs invasion at Playa Girón," García Márquez wrote. "Operation Carlota was not simply an expedition of professional soldiers; it was a war of the people."

After its troops were driven back across the border, the white-supremacist regime in South Africa, with backing and aid from the US government, helped initiate a bloody counterrevolutionary war against the new Angolan government—a war waged primarily by UNITA. UNITA's operations inside Angola received ample cross-border support from South African forces based in Namibia, including multiple further "incursions" by the apartheid regime. Faced with this situation, Angola requested that Cuba maintain its internationalist military mission in order to forestall other South African invasions. Over the next decade of stalemate, the war cost hundreds of thousands of Angolans their lives.

The impasse lasted until late 1987 when, in response to another full-scale South African invasion, the Cuban revolutionary leadership moved rapidly to reinforce Cuba's military in Angola.

The decisive battle to block the advancing South African forces was fought at the town of Cuito Cuanavale in southeastern Angola, where a group of Angolan and Cuban troops were surrounded. Over several months the town's defenders, led by the Cubans, held out against repeated South African thrusts.

Meanwhile, Cuban and Angolan reinforcements moved toward Cuito Cuanavale, and other units, including forces from SWAPO, simultaneously mounted a flanking operation in a broad arc southward toward Namibia.[3] By March 1988 strategic positions held by South African troops were themselves being threatened. Recognizing they could not take Cuito Cuanavale, the apartheid forces began a full-scale retreat toward the Namibian border.

Faced with growing mass struggles against apartheid rule at home as well, the South African regime sued for peace. In December 1988 an agreement was signed at the United Nations in New York between Angola, Cuba, and South Africa, in the presence of representatives of the US government. The accords called on South Africa to withdraw its forces from Angola and to recognize Namibia's independence. Immediately following the signing, Cuba and Angola jointly agreed to the withdrawal of Cuban forces.

The last Cuban troops left Angola in May 1991. More than two thousand Cuban internationalists had given their lives in the nearly sixteen-year mission.

"The crushing defeat of the racist army at Cuito Cuanavale was a victory for the whole of Africa!" said Nelson Mandela during a visit to Cuba in July 1991. Expressing the gratitude of the people of South Africa, Mandela underscored the contribution of the Cuban people to the overthrow of the apartheid regime itself. Cuito Cuanavale, he said, was "a turning point in the struggle to free the continent and our country from the scourge of apartheid!"[4]

---

1. See p. 127.

2. See p. 36.

3. See map, p. 43.

4. See p. 75.

PART I

Defending Angola's independence and sovereignty

CONSOLIDATING A POWERFUL BULWARK AGAINST APARTHEID SOUTH AFRICA

Fidel Castro
SEPTEMBER 1975

Excerpted from speech given at La Cabaña military base, Havana, September 12, 1975, to the first contingent of military instructors leaving for internationalist mission in Angola.

❧

... In any operation of this type, as you know, security of the mission's personnel requires maximum discretion. That's why the initial selection of the personnel was so important. And, as always in such circumstances, it's composed of volunteers. Of course, as you know, in our country there are many who are prepared to volunteer for any revolutionary and internationalist mission. . . .

Our army's missions in defense of the homeland are an obligation for everyone. You might also say that its missions in defense of revolutionary and internationalist causes are the duty of everyone

"The struggle by the patriots of Guinea-Bissau, Angola, and Mozambique led Portuguese colonialism to a crisis—first an international crisis of isolation, and finally to an internal crisis," said Fidel Castro in September 1975. **Above:** Crowds in Lisbon, April 1974, celebrate overthrow of hated dictatorship, in power for more than forty-five years. By November 1975, all of Portugal's colonies in Africa had won independence.

Reprinted from *La batalla de Cabinda* [The battle of Cabinda] by Ramón Espinosa Martín, army corps general of the Revolutionary Armed Forces of Cuba (Havana: Ediciones Verde Olivo, 2001).

as well. But when it comes to choosing a select group of men to carry out one of these missions we always prefer on principle that they be volunteers. I'm absolutely certain that there's not one officer, not one soldier in our Revolutionary Armed Forces who, having the chance to hear the commitment that you've made today and knowing the mission that you'll be carrying out—I'm completely sure that there's not one who'd let you head off alone.

I say this as a way of expressing our confidence in our combatants. They are men who have such a high level of consciousness—patriotic, revolutionary, and internationalist consciousness—that they're fully prepared to carry out any mission of this sort. And we have a very special appreciation for those compañeros who, when they are told of the need for a mission like this—in fact, more than that, when they don't even know what the mission is, just that it's classified as an internationalist mission—a very special appreciation for those compañeros who immediately declare they are willing to carry it out. . . .

In Portugal, a fascist government ruled for more than forty years. It carried out a ten-year war against those fighting for independence for the Portuguese colonies in Africa. But that very struggle by the patriots of Guinea-Bissau, Angola, and Mozambique led Portuguese colonialism and Portuguese fascism to a crisis. First an international crisis of isolation, of discredit to the government, and finally to an internal crisis.

That is, the Africans' fight for independence helped the Portuguese people—it was an element that helped give birth to the Portuguese revolution. Without the struggle in the Portuguese colonies in Africa, it's possible that the April 25 [1974] revolution in Portugal would never have occurred, or it would have taken much longer to develop. And events in Portugal, in turn, helped to accelerate the independence of the colonies in Africa.

The victory of the revolution in Portugal immediately posed the question of negotiations with the liberation movements in Africa and elsewhere. Guinea-Bissau acquired independence and Mozambique did so as well. In Angola, however, a special situation emerged.

There were three movements in Angola at that time. First, the MPLA (Popular Movement for the Liberation of Angola), the movement that organized the fight against the Portuguese and fought for the liberation of Angola for ten years.

As the struggle developed we received information that there were some individuals, led by Holden Roberto, who were connected to US imperialism—they were known by revolutionaries around the world as elements linked to imperialism. They barely participated in the struggle for Angola's liberation. In recent years, and increasingly so as the crisis of Portuguese imperialism deepened, they focused instead on organizing an army in the Congo, known today as Zaire.[1]

The Congo had been the scene of revolutionary struggles. [Patrice] Lumumba, a great leader, arose and was overthrown and later murdered by individuals in the service of neocolonialism and imperialism. The government that emerged was essentially the result of the crushing of the revolutionary process there. At times it has put forward a demagogic political line and made nationalist-sounding statements, but in reality it's one of Africa's reactionary governments. . . .

Zaire's intentions have been known for several years. They want to make use of elements led by Holden Roberto, who organized the so-called Angola Liberation Front [FNLA] and spent their time creating an army in Zaire while a war was being fought in Angola. The MPLA, on the other hand, was advancing the war with the aid of the progressive countries of the entire world.

Meanwhile, an army was being organized in Zaire. Angolan exiles living in the Congo were recruited. They claimed they had trained thousands of men, supposedly to fight the Portuguese. But it was clear that what was really being organized was an army that could take power *after* Angola won its independence, because during the war they didn't fight. They were trying to become strong enough to play a decisive role in the internal struggle after independence, and that's what happened.

The MPLA, for its part, had internal splits of rightist elements who then organized a third movement, known as UNITA, which has some

---

1. Two countries historically share the name Congo. Congo-Brazzaville (formally, Republic of the Congo), north of Angola, won independence from France in 1960. Congo (Democratic Republic of the Congo, known as Zaire from 1971 to 1997), northeast of Angola, won independence from Belgium in 1960.

"The Africans' fight for independence helped the Portuguese people give birth to the April 1974 revolution."

—*Fidel Castro, September 1975*

BAXTER SMITH/MILITANT

Top, right: Massive outpouring in Lisbon, May 1974, places demands on new government in wake of fall of dictatorship. **Above:** Demonstrators in New York, June 1974, join worldwide call for freedom for Portuguese colonies—the last in sub-Saharan Africa. **Right:** Celebrating independence in Luanda, Angola, November 1975.

Above: Oil platform in Cabinda belonging to US-owned Gulf Oil. Among the goals of Zaire's dictator Mobutu Sese Seko in backing the imperialist assault on Angola was to annex oil-rich Cabinda.

strength in the southern part of the country.

As soon as Portugal and the three liberation movements signed the accords—with supposed liberation movements; there was actually only one that was genuine—agreement was reached to create a provisional government that would have certain powers. At the beginning this provisional government was made up of the three forces, the MPLA, FNLA, and UNITA. This occurred in part because some African governments, eager to find a solution to the problem and avoid the consequences of a civil war, pressured the different movements, including the MPLA, to agree to it. One of the new government's responsibilities was to prepare conditions for full independence on November 11, 1975. The Portuguese gave weapons to each of the three movements.

That alliance couldn't last long and at a certain point it broke apart. It seems that those in the FNLA committed a series of abuses and crimes during the period of the unity government. According to what we've been told, their actions created great hostility in the population. They were strong above all near the border with Zaire. They began to move the troops they were training in Zaire to Angola, in the northern zone, and occupied an area there.

There's something that partially explains the dispute over Angola. The fact is, the country has a small territory to the north—a small area separate from the rest of Angola, called Cabinda. Cabinda is located north of the mouth of the Congo River, and is separated from the rest of Angola not only by the river, but also by a strip of land that's part of Zaire....[2]

In the last few years oil was discovered in this small part of Angolan territory, apparently in abundant quantities. They're in the first stages of production and I've been told that they have already pumped several million tons. This has become a source of conflict that has drawn the interest of monopoly corporations in Europe and the United States; it's an element in the situation created in Angola, given the present difficult situation in the world with oil....

Cabinda now is among the regions with important oil reserves. It's quite possible that Zaire is thinking about taking over the territory, and with it Angola's oil. The issue of oil is a constant thread throughout this struggle.

Cabinda has a relatively small population, about eighty thousand. It's currently under the complete control of the MPLA. But its isolation from the rest of the country makes it a possible target at a given point.... At the moment there's no fighting there, ... but there has been fighting ... in the rest of Angola's territory in recent months, especially in the north, and also in part of the south, where UNITA's people are. The MPLA tried to neutralize UNITA so it could confront the FNLA in the north, but disagreements came up and UNITA began to fight the MPLA.

These are the main features of the political situation. What has become clear in recent months? That the MPLA has the capacity to react and fight. At the outset, the army from Zaire, apparently well armed with armored vehicles and other equipment, advanced from the north and approached Luanda. At times it seemed that that reactionary army organized in Zaire might dominate the situation. But the combatants of the MPLA, which is a very progressive revolutionary organization, with people fighting for ideas, reacted and contained the offensive. And at a point some forty kilometers from the capital, the MPLA not only resisted but

---

2. The European imperialist powers divided Africa among themselves at a conference in Berlin in 1885. To give the Belgian monarchy access to the sea for it's landlocked Congo colony, a sliver was cut through Portugal's holdings. As a result, Angola's northern province of Cabinda came to be geographically separated from the rest of the country.

began to take back territory as well.

When the FNLA carried out another offensive, just recently, it was reported they got within fifteen or twenty kilometers of Luanda. When they were fifteen kilometers away, the MPLA responded again and drove them back to Caxito, some forty or fifty kilometers away. According to recent reports, the MPLA has taken Caxito and is advancing north. In the south they confronted forces from UNITA and there too . . . contained them, took several positions, and have since kept them at bay.

The current situation is that the MPLA holds twelve provinces . . . in Angola, in addition to Cabinda. Reactionary forces control some provinces in the north and a few in the south. The majority of the country is in the hands of the MPLA. But the political factor is the most important thing: the population of Angola supports the MPLA.

The FNLA has won the hatred of the population. As I mentioned, they are said to have carried out all kinds of misdeeds, extortions, and crimes during the period of the provisional three-power government. The MPLA, on the other hand, has based itself on the masses. They have had the organization, the discipline, and an approach toward the population that won them support. The situation among the people is very favorable toward the MPLA and that is a very important point.

In terms of weapons, the MPLA has arms from the time of the war of liberation, others they were given by the Portuguese at the time of the cease-fire and the creation of the provisional government, and some the Soviets sent. The MPLA was backed by the socialist countries, by progressive forces throughout the world. The MPLA is part of the Nonaligned movement and has had strong international support. They are considered the most revolutionary force, the truly progressive revolutionary force of Angola.

The Soviets recently sent.

26 armored vehicles;

32 GRAD-1PS—the *granizos* [mobile multiple-rocket launchers];

12 76-mm cannons;

3,216 RPG-7 bazookas;

39 82-mm mortars;

4 antiaircraft batteries with 23-mm cannons;

44 ZCU antiaircraft guns;

298 machine guns;

2,899 AKM rifles;

84 radio transmitters; and

10,000 uniforms, both military and civilian.

I am giving you these facts because you are going to the territory of Angola below Cabinda and it's important you know what types of weapons the MPLA has recently received. They have a lot of really powerful armaments.

We assume they don't have much experience with the weapons, but we have no doubt that one way or another they are using them with some effectiveness. For example, during the FNLA's latest offensive against Luanda with armored vehicles, it's clear that rocket launchers were used against them. And we've been told that the MPLA used bazookas and antiaircraft cannons in a number of battles. So they have some capacity to assimilate and use the weapons even though, of course, as you may assume, they don't have great military experience and they don't have in-depth knowledge of how to use them.

It wasn't easy for the weapons to get there because of the special situation. There are two states within Angola—the Portuguese state, which still has troops there, and the new state that is being formed, made up of revolutionaries. The Portuguese are armed and remain in their barracks. The revolutionaries are waging their war well armed.

The Portuguese forces in Cabinda have shown a fairly positive attitude toward the MPLA. In the rest of Angola, according to reports, there are many Portuguese officials who are reactionary. It's not that they have intervened—although there have been some incidents with the MPLA from time to time—but there are many reactionary officers commanding Portuguese troops. It's clear that the troops themselves have no interest in fighting.

What is the main mission of our volunteer detachment? According to the agreements we've reached with the MPLA, it's to create a leadership team, a general staff that can advise them in the present struggle. Secondly, it's to create four military schools in four separate areas. These schools will have about two hundred [Cuban] men each, three in lower Angola and one in Cabinda.

The personnel going to Cabinda are not here today precisely because, for security reasons, we don't want that group, which is going later, to know the facts you're learning today. That's why they aren't at this meeting. Gathered here are members of the mission's general staff, the medical personnel, and the personnel for the three military schools in lower Angola.

For your part, when you get to Angola you shouldn't speak to anyone about issues in Cabinda, or about the troops going there. I'm telling you about this now so you'll have an overall view, so that you know there will be combatants in Cabinda who will be far from you, because, as I've said, they'll be in a territory separate from the rest of the country.

The units that go to the different schools will have responsibility for training and organizing the Angolans. There will be a total of five thousand men at the schools. In effect, when you get there and link up with the Angolans, we'll have the basis for a new army. In addition to the combatants deployed on the various fronts, we'll be creating what we might call a reserve force of five thousand men. Our first task is to train these men.

This structure is something we've discussed with the compañeros of the MPLA. Initially they were thinking of small groups of Cubans carrying out training tasks in many difficult places. We suggested that instead of dispersing the Cuban forces we should group them in a series of important points, to create large schools. Why did we want this? Because it's much easier to lead and organize our forces this way, rather than having them dispersed. More importantly, it's much safer because in a worst-case scenario a unit of sixty or seventy Cubans is a respectable force.

We who were part of the guerrilla campaign never had seventy men with the kind of military knowledge and weapons that you'll have. Seventy men with automatic rifles, mortars, bazookas, and antitank and antiaircraft cannons can face any situation. This includes the worst variant, a situation in which there's nobody left in the group but Cubans. Any one of these groups is strong enough to confront any military situation that might arise in the kind of war that's under way there.

There are no aircraft in action in Angola, so the antiaircraft machine guns can be used for ground combat. You can't use massed tanks in that terrain; there are too many rivers and other natural obstacles. Whatever tank force Holden Roberto might bring down from the north can be wiped out by a small unit with mortars, bazookas, and antitank cannons, in a well-chosen position.

That's why, with the security of our personnel in mind, we proposed the approach of concentrating the schools so we can concentrate our personnel.

Photos: Cuban and Angolan combatants at military school in Cabinda province—one of four set up at request of MPLA in September–October 1975 with help from first detachment of Cuban volunteers.

This gives them the capacity to fight under any circumstances.

I was talking about the worst variant, the worst situation that might develop at the beginning, when the schools aren't yet well organized, when the personnel aren't yet prepared or trained.... If it turns out that no such necessity is posed, new contingents will be trained, and then the next and the next. That's how a new Angolan army will be organized. That's how the situation will evolve in the best of circumstances, as it's doing now for the MPLA.

It's possible the MPLA will defeat the FNLA first, then UNITA, and there won't be any need for the direct participation of the schools, or of the Cuban personnel. But circumstances could arise in which one of the schools would be called upon to support an operation or defend a region. In that case, the school with its Cuban personnel would take part in military operations.

The Cuban general staff group can provide important advice, of course, and the medical personnel, wherever they might be, will have their hands full taking care of the Cuban personnel, the school personnel, the Angolan personnel, and the population. Wherever a doctor shows up, as you well know, his services will be needed right away.

Each school will have its own weapons:

9 82-mm mortars;

7 75-mm recoilless cannon;

18 RPG-7 bazookas;

6 antiaircraft cannon.

All Cuban personnel will have their own AKM automatic rifles. The Angolan troops will have Czech semiautomatic rifles, vz-52s I think.[3] We haven't sent the AKs, not because we want to deny them to the schools—the Cuban personnel will be sent with AKs—it's just that we, in compliance with the military agreements, cannot freely provide the Soviet arms we have received. So we

---

3. The AKM, an automatic rifle with a 30-round clip, was used by the armed forces of the Soviet Union from 1959 to 1974, when it was largely replaced by a lighter, faster-firing model. The vz-52, a rifle with a 10-round clip, was used by the armed forces of Czechoslovakia from 1952 to 1959.

sent Chinese artillery and other types of non-Soviet weapons....

Of course it has been essential to include some Soviet weapons, but we have kept them to a minimum in order not to violate the agreements on the supply of arms. That why we're sending the Czech rifles. In the first shipments we're going to send twelve thousand.

If we add together the weapons—those they already had, those the Soviets sent, those the Portuguese handed over, and those we sent—there are probably enough for twenty thousand men. Some rifles they got from the Portuguese use FAL bullets, which we can supply.... Each school will have enough weapons to defend itself and to carry out a military operation of any character. We assume those weapons should stay in the schools—unless a situation arises in which the students and the Cuban personnel in the school have to go into combat—so that when one contingent leaves another can come for training.

There was another occasion in which a Cuban detachment carried out a mission in solidarity with the people of Africa—that was in the Congo several years ago. One of the things that had the greatest impact on our combatants then was the clash between different cultures and ways of thinking. The Cubans were confronted with the culture of the people of the area—their lack of organization, of discipline. They also had to deal with the combatants' religious beliefs, their superstitions. This had an unfortunate impact, creating pessimism.

I'm warning you about this because I believe it's one of the fundamental questions—of course I'm speaking of a very different situation. It was the practical effect of those superstitions that was so traumatic for our combatants—the people who went into combat, the way they would pray if they didn't go, all those things.

The example I'm referring to is very different. There was no political organization like the MPLA, guided by revolutionary principles, by progressive political views, with educated cadres. The impression I have from here is that these combatants, the Angolan patriots, are much more advanced in organization and political culture than were those in the Congo, the ones we went to help. This is the conclusion we have drawn. They are much better organized and much better educated politically. We think they can become good combatants.

I'm giving you this advice, however, because you'll come up against different things, different customs—things you never encountered in the environment in which you were born and educated.

A man's attitude to war depends on his cultural level and political development. In many African countries that were enslaved, colonized, and living in tribal conditions, you won't find exactly the same level of culture or the same political development as you find in our country. And one of your missions is to make good soldiers out of these men, to train them, to give them confidence.

Above all, it's very important that you don't fall into a tendency to underestimate any African combatant. You have to be very alert to this. If you meet difficulties, if you find cultural backwardness, if you find superstition, you must learn how to take up those questions with great patience, with great understanding, and with great intelligence.

One thing none of you should ever fall into is an attitude of scorn or contempt for an African combatant. I would say of all our norms and principles, the most important is the following: you should approach the men who will be under your leadership, who will be instructed and trained by you . . . with an absolutely understanding frame of mind, an absolutely fraternal attitude. You must develop the best relations with those men.

This point is of the greatest importance. Understanding it is the essence, the guarantee of successfully carrying through the mission. And I can tell you now, we have a good impression of the Angolan combatants, but you, in your thinking, must be prepared to run into obstacles, problems, and superstitions.

Your mission is to make soldiers out of these men, help them develop a new culture, a new attitude, a knowledge of what it means to be a soldier, a capacity to react and to act as different military tasks present themselves. Don't ever forget this in the relationship between you and the men you will be dealing with. If at any moment an Angolan compañero sees an attitude of arrogance or of superiority in you, that would have very negative consequences. They should never get the impression that you consider yourselves superior to them; they should never have the impression that they are being looked down upon or scorned by you. From the psychological point of view, this is a key question.

Don't expect to find in Angola the degree of organization we have in this country today. You'll have to face shortcomings, disorganization, obstacles. This mission would have no special importance if it were an easy one, if you were going to arrive in Angola and find a people like today's Cuban people. They will have to go through a lengthy period of struggle, and of cultural and political education, before becoming a people at the level of the people of Cuba today. That is to say, you aren't going to work in ideal conditions, in a perfect setting. You must assume that the work will have to be done under difficult conditions.

I believe that many of you have experience in training men, in instructing men, and I believe that you are certain that, no matter how difficult the circumstances may be, you will fulfill correctly your missions as instructors, as teachers, and possibly even as leaders in combat of those Angolan patriots. Under these conditions there are different dangers. I said before that perhaps you will not have to take part in combat, that perhaps the present fighters of the MPLA will be able to control the situation . . . but perhaps at some point they will need your direct support.

Other potential dangers: that troops from Zaire intervene, that regular troops invade the country. In a situation such as that, you will without doubt find yourselves involved in the fighting. There are reports, for example, that South African troops have penetrated into some border regions from the south. . . . If there is an intervention by South African troops, you will have to intervene.

A less likely situation: that the internal situation in Portugal gets more complicated, that reactionary and rightist elements take power in Portugal, try to maintain domination over Angola, and intervene in support of the FNLA or another of those organizations. This is not very likely. It would be hard for anyone to convince the troops there to fight a war. But in this hypothetical case, it's almost certain that the schools and the Angolans would have to intervene.

The compañeros in charge of this mission and the compañeros of the political staff will keep you as well informed as possible about the course of events and the situation in general, the news of what is happening in Cabinda, in any area, in any front, the evolution of the international situation.

With this mission that you are going to carry out, we shouldn't only think that we are acting in accord with our principles, in accord with our duty of international solidarity, but rather that with this act of solidarity we will be expressing the feelings and the interests of all the progressive sectors of the world. If at some point they start to say that there are Cubans in Africa.... well, that won't be a bad thing. It's not that we're going to be announcing it, we're not going to announce it, but I'm certain that the simple fact that Cubans are side by side with the MPLA will inspire more respect from the reactionary elements of Africa. And there are a large number of progressive countries and governments that sympathize with and support the MPLA: the Soviet Union and all the countries of Eastern Europe support the MPLA, Algeria supports the MPLA, the revolutionary movements of Mozambique and Guinea-Bissau support the MPLA, the majority of the Nonaligned nations support the MPLA. In Angola, the MPLA represents the progressive cause of the world.

It's extremely important that Angola not fall into the hands of the reactionaries and the colonists, because of the three Portuguese colonies, Guinea-Bissau is solid, Mozambique is solid, and Angola we can help to become solid, in revolutionary hands. It is of paramount importance that none of these three countries fall into the hands of colonialism or reaction. It is a question of great strategic significance for Africa. If Mobutu and the reactionaries were to gain control of Angola, they would be in a very strong position, reaction and imperialism would hold a very strong position in Africa.

Africa still has very serious problems. In time they'll have to deal with the question of racism, of South Africa, which is one of the biggest problems the continent has. The two great problems were Portuguese colonialism and the racism in South Africa, where a few million keep fourteen million Africans oppressed. For all the peoples of Africa, South Africa is a problem that touches the most sensitive nerve.

Consolidation of the Angolan revolutionary movement strengthens progressive Africa. It strengthens all the revolutionary governments in Africa and it could become a powerful bulwark against South Africa. This is why it's important to come to the aid of the Angolan revolution. It is of major importance for Africa, for the world, for the progressive world movement. It's why this is a task of truly historic importance.

As our armed forces fulfill these revolutionary duties, it increases their experience, their strength, and their combative spirit. The brigade that was in Syria, for example, gained a great deal of experience there in modern warfare, modern tactics, and the effectiveness of different weapons—a rich experience that our Revolutionary Armed Forces has incorporated as its own.[4]

You all have chosen the honorable road of the revolutionary professional soldier; you have studied in the schools and academies for many years. The mission of our armed forces transcends our national borders. When Cuban soldiers are trained, they are trained to fight in Cuba should that be necessary. But if their capabilities and knowledge are needed to serve alongside those of a sister nation in Latin America or in Africa or Asia, they are ready to serve wherever they are needed.

For those of us who in one way or another participated in the revolution, in the defeat of the forces of repression, in the defeat of the old army, it's a great satisfaction to see this new army that has arisen from the ranks of the revolution and shows such mettle and spirit. It is a great satisfaction to see the efforts of the Moncada, *Granma*, and Sierra Maestra combatants reflected today in this superb group of new soldiers of the Cuban Revolution, of our country's new combatants. It is a great satisfaction to see the same attitude, generosity, spirit, willingness to fight and sacrifice, and noble ability to step forward when needed for a just cause.

We are proud of you. If we may say so, many of the compañeros present here are actually sorry that we can't go with you. We regret not having the

---

4. At the request of the government in Damascus, Cuba sent a volunteer tank battalion to Syria in October 1973. At the time Syrian and Egyptian forces were fighting a war against the Israeli army to try to retake the Golan Heights and territory in the Sinai desert, occupied by Israel since the 1967 war. While the Cuban battalion, which later grew to a regiment, did not see combat, it did organize fortification of Syrian defenses, helping deter further Israeli aggression. The unit remained in Syria until February 1975.

chance to carry out a mission like this.

I see that many of you, the vast majority, are young compañeros. That means it will be a great experience in your lives, a great opportunity to carry out an important mission, to serve the world revolutionary movement, to achieve something worthy of national commendation.

We aren't going to say this mission is free of danger. The mission does present dangers, it does have risks. Depending on how the situation develops these can be significant. But we are sure that will not shake your resolve, being the revolutionary soldiers, the professional military men that you are.

And as you leave tomorrow, you should keep uppermost in mind that we are all brothers, that your parents are our parents, your brothers and sisters are our brothers and sisters, your children our children, the children of the revolution. If while carrying out the mission one of you should lose your life, not one loved one will be left uncared for, not one child will be left orphaned. That is exactly what the revolution, the great family of revolutionaries, the socialist country, stands for.

A new future has opened for all of us, an opportunity has opened to realize our deepest feelings, our aspirations, our vocation. You have been given the chance to be soldiers, to be officers and, best of all, to be revolutionaries and to know that when our country needs you it can count on you.

Along with our warm feelings of affection, our confidence also goes with you, the confidence of our party and the confidence of our glorious Revolutionary Armed Forces. We know your qualities, the qualities of the men who are going to carry out this mission, and we are absolutely certain you will do so successfully and victoriously.

¡Patria o muerte! [Homeland or death!]
¡Venceremos! [We will win!]

AFRICAN BLOOD FLOWS THROUGH OUR VEINS
Fidel Castro
DECEMBER 1975

Excerpted from speech given to mass rally of more than one million in Havana, December 22, 1975, following the close of the First Congress of the Communist Party of Cuba.

...And now it is Angola that is the source of friction. The imperialists seek to prevent us from aiding our Angolan brothers. But we must tell the Yankees to bear in mind that we are a Latin-American nation and a Latin-African nation as well. [*Prolonged applause*]

African blood flows freely through our veins. [*Applause*] Many of our ancestors came as slaves from Africa to this land. As slaves they struggled a great deal. They fought as members of the Liberating Army of Cuba. We're brothers and sisters of the people of Africa and we're ready to fight on their behalf! [*Applause*]

Racial discrimination existed in our country. Is there anyone who doesn't know this, who doesn't remember it? Many public parks had separate walks for blacks and for whites. Is there anyone who doesn't recall that African descendants were barred from many places, from recreation centers and schools? Is there anyone who has forgotten that racial discrimination was prevalent in all aspects of work and study?

And, today, who are the representatives, the symbols of the most hateful and inhuman form of racial discrimination? The South African fascists and racists. And Yankee imperialism, without scruples of any kind, has launched South African mercenary troops in an attempt to crush Angola's independence and is now outraged by our help to Angola, our support for Africa and our defense of Africa. In keeping with the duties rooted in our principles, our ideology, our convictions and our very own blood, we shall defend Angola and Africa! [*Applause and shouts of "Cuba, Angola, united they will win!"*] And when we say defend, we mean it in the strict sense of the word. And when we say struggle, we mean it also in the strict sense of the word. [*Applause*]

Let the South African racists and the Yankee imperialists be warned. We are part of the world revolutionary movement, and in Africa's struggle against racists and imperialists, we'll stand, without any hesitation, side by side with the peoples of Africa. [*Applause*]

Only cynics would dare to condemn our support for Angola while marching upon that heroic people shoulder to shoulder with South African fascists; South Africa, a region where three million whites oppress 14 million blacks, wants to impose its policy on Rhodesia [Zimbabwe since 1979], as it is doing, and on the rest of black Africa. But black Africa will not stand for it, will not tolerate it. Imperialists and reactionaries underestimate the peoples; mercenaries are in the habit of doing as they please, of marching in with their tanks and cannon to overwhelm defenseless people. They've already tried it here in Girón, and that's just what they're trying to do in Angola. But Angolans are not defenseless! [*Applause*]

And [US president] Ford is complaining. Ford is hurling threats. Not really threats. He is just saying that the hypothetical and abstract possibilities of improving relations will be canceled.[1] Ford should instead apologize to the Revolutionary Government of Cuba for the scores of assassination attempts prepared by the CIA for many years against

---

The full text of this speech appears in the January 11, 1976, issue of *Granma Weekly Review*.

various leaders of the Revolution. [*Applause*]

The Government of Cuba has the right to expect explanations from the imperialist government of the United States and to receive apologies for the horrendous and macabre assassination attempts plotted against leaders of the Cuban Revolution, attesting to their degree of civilization, or rather their degree of barbarity, and showing their true colors as criminals. They have put technology and science at the service of murder. And for years on end, in an unscrupulous, foul and indecent manner, that government has dedicated itself to planning the assassination of revolutionary Cuban leaders.[2]

What we want from Ford is not the cancelation of his hypothetical hopes or possibilities for an improvement of relations with Cuba, but apologies for the shameful, hateful, and disgraceful crimes which the Government of the United States prepared against leaders of the Cuban Revolution. [*Applause and shouts of "Fidel, hit the Yankees hard!"*]

Our people have never failed to fulfill their internationalist commitment. Our people have maintained a policy consistent with their principles throughout their history.

What do the imperialists think? Do they think that since we are interested in social and economic progress we are going to sell out [*Shouts of "No!"*] in exchange for their purchase of a little bit of sugar and sale of cheap goods? [*Shouts of "No!"*] What do the imperialists think? Don't they realize that the world is changing and that the times of blackmail and impositions on this country are over? This country on which they imposed the Platt Amendment,[3] as well as scores of turncoats and treacherous rulers. Are they going to impose something else on this country, where a revolution has triumphed? No! They are mistaken. And we have said it before; although economic relations with the United States may be useful to our country, these relations will never be reestablished on the basis of giving up one single iota of our principles. [*Applause*]

We think that our entire people agree on this. [*Shouts of "Yes!"*] And I think that not just this generation but future ones will also be in agreement.

If imperialism cannot improve relations with Cuba, since capitalism is incapable of respecting international rules; if capitalism is incapable of respecting the freedom and sovereignty of other peoples, that's their problem. Let them give up capitalism in order to solve their problem. But they can't very well ask us to give up socialism and proletarian internationalism [*Shouts of "No!"*] and our ideology. [*Shouts of "No!"*]

It is not we who are obstinately opposed to having normal relations. But if capitalism, mighty and authoritarian, doesn't want anything to do with us, not even to speak with or look at this small nation, then we'll wait until capitalism is wiped out in the United States.

We defend peaceful coexistence and relations with other countries. If they are unwilling to have relations with us, that's their business. Fortunately, we don't need them for anything. [*Applause*]

Dear compañeros, we hadn't met in Plaza of the Revolution for quite some time. Today we meet to celebrate a happy event; our First Congress, which has truly been a historical event. And whenever we get together on this spot, we cannot but feel admiration for our people, their strength, cohesion, enthusiasm, and ideology.

---

1. On December 20, 1975, President Gerald Ford threatened to end US-Cuban talks about family visits and other steps to normalize US-Cuban relations, saying that "the action by the Cuban Government in sending combat forces to Angola destroys any opportunity for improvement of relations with the United States." At a January 15, 1976, press conference, Cuban president Fidel Castro responded: "It is not that Cuba reject[s] the ideal of improving relations with the United States. . . . What we do not accept are humiliating conditions—the absurd price that the United States apparently would have us pay for an improvement of relations." The talks ended in February 1976.

2. According to Cuba's Ministry of Interior, between 1959 and 1999, there were 637 assassination attempts against Fidel Castro organized by the US government or US-backed counterrevolutionary groups.

3. The Platt Amendment was imposed by US imperialism on the 1901 Cuban constitution during Washington's military occupation at that time. Named after a US Senator, the "amendment" established Washington's "right" to intervene in Cuba whenever the US rulers deemed it necessary to guarantee "maintenance of a government adequate for the protection of life, property, and individual," and authorized establishment of the now infamous US naval base at Guantánamo Bay, which continues to this day to be occupied against the will of the Cuban people.

On more than one occasion, we, the privileged heirs of the struggles of generations of Cubans, have had the pleasure and happiness of watching a rally like this one. Often we've had the opportunity of feeling from deep in our hearts an infinite love and admiration for our people.

Today I only want to tell you—fully convinced of and trusting that our path, broad and beautiful, is unfolding before our very eyes—that this rally, this meeting between the Party and the masses, between the Central Committee and the masses, is one of the most extraordinary events in our revolutionary process and one of the happiest days of our lives.

¡Patria o muerte! [Homeland or death!]

¡Venceremos! [We will win!]

ANGOLA: AN AFRICAN GIRÓN

Fidel Castro
APRIL 1976

Excerpted from speech given in Havana's Karl Marx theater, April 19, 1976, commemorating the fifteenth anniversary of the Cuban victory at the Bay of Pigs (Playa Girón).

... In commemorating this, the fifteenth anniversary of the heroic, glorious victory at Girón, our people have an additional reason to be proud, one which constitutes their finest expression of internationalism and transcends the boundaries of this continent: the historical victory of the people of Angola, [*Prolonged applause*] to whom we offered the generous and unlimited solidarity of our revolution.

At Girón, African blood was shed, that of the selfless descendants of a people who were slaves before they became workers, and who were exploited workers before they became masters of their homeland. And in Africa, together with the blood of the heroic fighters of Angola, Cuban blood, that of the sons of Martí, Maceo, and Agramonte, that of the heirs to

Above: Playa Girón, Cuba, April 1961: Cuban volunteer militiamen celebrate defeat of US-organized invasion at Bay of Pigs. "For the Yankee imperialists, Angola represents an African Girón," said Fidel Castro in April 1976. "One of the most brilliant pages in the history of the liberation of black Africa was written."

The full text of this speech is available in *Fidel Castro Speeches: Cuba's Internationalist Foreign Policy 1975–80* (Pathfinder, 1981).

the internationalist tradition set by Máximo Gómez and Che Guevara,[1] also flowed. [*Prolonged applause*] Those who once enslaved man and sent him to America perhaps never imagined that one of those peoples who received the slaves would one day send their fighters to struggle for freedom in Africa.

The victory in Angola was the twin sister of the victory at Girón. [*Applause*] For the Yankee imperialists, Angola represents an African Girón. At one time we said that imperialism had suffered its great defeats in the month of April: Girón, Vietnam, Cambodia, etc.[2] This time the defeat came in March. On the twenty-seventh of that month, when the last South African soldiers crossed the Namibian border, after a retreat of more than seven hundred kilometers, one of the most brilliant pages in the liberation of black Africa was written.

[President Gerald] Ford and [Secretary of State Henry] Kissinger are irritated by the defeat. And like two little thundering Jupiters, they have made terrible threats against Cuba.

Ford, in an election campaign rally in Miami, competing for the votes of the Cuban counterrevolutionary colony with his rival Reagan, who, to be sure, is much more reactionary, called the prime minister of Cuba an international outlaw because of the aid our people gave to Angola. Even some United States press columnists were surprised to hear such epithets emerge from the illustrious mouth of Mr. Ford. Moreover, perhaps as one indication of Ford's low level of development, which is becoming proverbial, he declared on one occasion that Cuba's action in Angola was similar to what happened in Ethiopia in Mussolini's time.[3] And later on, not satisfied with that most original historical simile, he compared the events in Angola to Hitler's dismemberment of Czechoslovakia after Munich.[4]

---

1. See glossary for José Martí, Antonio Maceo, Ignacio Agramonte, Máximo Gómez, and Che Guevara.

2. A US-organized invasion was defeated at Playa Girón (the Bay of Pigs) on April 19, 1961. The US-backed dictatorships in South Vietnam and Cambodia fell in April 1975 and US personnel fled both countries.

3. In October 1935 troops of the Italian fascist government invaded and occupied Ethiopia.

4. In March 1939 German troops occupied Czechoslovakia following the signing, six months earlier, of the Munich pact with the British, French, and Italian governments.

The war in Angola was really Kissinger's war. Against the advice of some of his closest collaborators, he insisted on carrying out covert operations to liquidate the MPLA through the counterrevolutionary FNLA and UNITA groups, with the support of white mercenaries, Zaire, and South Africa. It is said that the CIA actually warned him that such clandestine operations could not be kept secret. Aside from the fact that from the time it was founded the FNLA was supported by the CIA, a fact now publicly acknowledged, the United States invested tens of millions of dollars from the spring of 1975 on to supply arms and instructors to the counterrevolutionary, secessionist Angolan groups. Instigated by the United States, regular troops from Zaire entered Angolan territory in the summer of that same year, while South African military forces occupied the Cunene area in the month of August and sent arms and instructors to UNITA bands.

At that time there wasn't a single Cuban instructor in Angola. The first material aid and the first Cuban instructors reached Angola at the beginning of October, at the request of the MPLA, when Angola was being openly invaded by foreign forces. However, no Cuban military unit had been sent to Angola to participate di-

"Those who once enslaved man and sent him to America never imagined that one of those peoples who received the slaves would one day send their fighters to struggle for freedom in Africa," said Fidel Castro. **Above:** Cuban and Angolan forces on patrol at Ruacaná, near Namibian border where, in March 1976, last South African soldier crossed after retreating more than 700 kilometers.

Celebrating Angola's independence in Cabinda, December 1975, following defeat of invasion by troops of US-backed regime in Zaire.

rectly in the fight, nor was that projected.

On October 23 [1975], also instigated by the United States, South African regular army troops, supported by tanks and artillery, invaded Angolan territory across the Namibian border and penetrated deeply into the country, advancing between sixty and seventy kilometers a day. On November 3, they had penetrated more than five hundred kilometers into Angola, meeting their first resistance on the outskirts of Benguela, from the personnel of a recently organized school for Angolan recruits and from their Cuban instructors, who had virtually no means for halting the attack by South African tanks, infantry, and artillery.

On November 5, 1975, at the request of the MPLA, the leadership of our party decided to send with great urgency a battalion of regular troops with antitank weapons [*Applause*] to help the Angolan patriots resist the invasion of the South African racists. This was the first Cuban troop unit sent to Angola. When it arrived in the country, the foreign interventionists in the north were twenty-five kilometers from Luanda, their 140-millimeter artillery was bombing the suburbs of the capital, and the South African fascists had already penetrated more than seven hundred kilometers into the south from the Namibian border, while Cabinda was heroically defended by MPLA fighters and a handful of Cuban instructors.

I do not mean to relate the events of the Angolan war, the recent developments of which are generally known to everyone, but rather to point out the occasion, the form, and the circumstances in which our aid began. These facts now form part of history.[5]

The enemy has talked about the number of Cubans in Angola. It is sufficient to say that once the struggle began, Cuba sent the men and the weapons necessary to win that struggle. [*Applause*] To give due honor to our people, we must say that hundreds of thousands of combatants from our regular troops and reserves were ready to fight alongside their Angolan brothers. [*Applause*]

Our losses were minimal. In spite of the fact that the war was fought on four fronts and that our fighters fought alongside the heroic MPLA soldiers in the liberation of almost a million square kilometers [*Applause*] that had been occupied by the interventionists and their accomplices, fewer Cuban soldiers were killed in action in over four months of fighting in Angola than in the three days of fighting at Girón.[6] [*Applause*]

Cuba alone bears the responsibility for taking that decision. The USSR had always helped the peoples of the Portuguese colonies in their struggle for independence, provided besieged Angola with basic aid in military equipment, and collaborated with us when imperialism had cut off practically all our air routes to Africa, but it never requested that a single Cuban be sent to that country. The USSR is extraordinarily respectful and careful in its relations with Cuba. A decision of that nature could only be made by our own party. [*Applause*]

Ford and Kissinger lie to the people of the United States and to world public opinion when they try to place the responsibility for Cuba's action in solidarity with Angola on the Soviet Union.

Ford and Kissinger lie when they seek to blame

---

5. For a complete account of this stage of the Cuban mission in Angola, see "Operation Carlota," pp. 123–35.

6. One hundred fifty-seven Cuban combatants were killed in defeating the April 1961 invasion at the Bay of Pigs (Playa Girón).

"**No country of black Africa has anything to fear from Cuba's armed forces. We are a Latin-African people—enemies of colonialism, racism, and apartheid, which US imperialism aids and protects.**"

—Fidel Castro, April 1976

GRANMA

Above: Conakry, Guinea, March 1976. From right, Angolan president Agostinho Neto, Fidel Castro, Guinea president Sékou Touré, and Luis Cabral, president of Guinea-Bissau, at meeting to coordinate efforts to defeat South African aggression against Angola.
Below: Angolan and Cuban troops celebrate victory over US-backed Zairean and FNLA forces that had been pushed back across northern border, April 1976.

the Congress of the United States for the defeat of the interventionists in Angola because Congress failed to authorize new funds for the FNLA and UNITA counterrevolutionary groups. Congress made those decisions on December 16, 18, and 19. By that time, the CIA had already supplied large amounts in arms. Zairean troops had been repulsed in Luanda, Cabinda had been saved, the South Africans were contained and demoralized on the banks of the Queve River [near Sumbe], and no shipment of arms from the CIA would have changed the already inexorable course of events. Today the arms would be in the hands of the revolutionary forces, like many of those the CIA supplied earlier.

Ford and Kissinger lie to the people of the United States, and especially to the black population of that country, when they hide the fact that the fascist and racist troops of South Africa criminally invaded Angolan territory long before Cuba sent any regular units of soldiers there.

There are some other lies on the part of Ford and Kissinger in relation to Angola that need not be analyzed now. Ford and Kissinger know perfectly well that everything I say is true.

In this solemn commemoration ceremony, I am not going to say what I think of the insolent epithets Ford has used in his political campaign through the South of the United States and of other cynical aspects of his imperial policy; I will confine myself, for now, to replying that he is a common liar. [*Applause*]

True, events in Angola resemble those of Ethiopia, but in reverse. In Angola, the imperialists, the racists, the aggressors symbolized by the CIA, the South African troops, and the white mercenaries did not win victory nor did they occupy the country; victory was won by those who were attacked, by the revolutionaries, by the heroic black people of Angola. [*Applause*]

True, events in Angola resemble those of Czechoslovakia after Munich, but also in reverse: the people who were attacked received the solidarity of the revolutionary movement, and the imperialists and racists could not dismember the country or divide up its wealth or assassinate its finest sons and daughters. Angola is united, its territory is unified, and today it is a bulwark of liberty and dignity in Africa. The swastika of the South African racists does not fly over the palace of Luanda. [*Applause*]

We advise Mr. Ford to study a bit of true history and draw the correct conclusions from its lessons.

With the imperialist defeat in Angola, Mr. Kissinger scarcely has time enough to run from place to place whipping up fear of the Cuban Revolution. Some days ago he traveled through half a dozen Latin American countries and now he has announced a new trip to several countries in Africa, a continent he never deigned to look at before his African Girón.

No Latin American country, whatever its social system, will have anything to fear from the armed forces of Cuba. It is our deepest conviction that each people must be free to build their own destiny; that each people and only the people of each country must and will make their own revolution. The government of Cuba has never thought of taking revolution to any nation of this hemisphere with the arms of its military units. Such an idea would be absurd and ridiculous. Nor is it Cuba who stole the major part of its territory from Mexico, landed forty thousand marines to crush the revolution in Santo Domingo, occupies part of Panamanian territory, oppresses a Latin people in Puerto Rico, plans assassinations of foreign leaders, or exploits the wealth and natural resources of any people in this hemisphere.

No country of black Africa has anything to fear from Cuban military personnel. We are a Latin-African people—enemies of colonialism, neocolonialism, racism, and apartheid, which Yankee imperialism aids and protects.

They say that Kissinger wants to meet in Africa with the representatives of the liberation movements of that continent. Anything is possible in black Africa after the Girón of Angola. [*Applause*] But what kind of hypocritical, cynical, and sanctimonious words can Kissinger speak to the African liberation movements, to the representatives of the oppressed peoples of Rhodesia [Zimbabwe since 1979], Namibia, and South Africa—he who represents the empire that unscrupulously supported Portuguese colonialism and today aids, protects, and supports with economic and political means the South African and Rhodesian racists, in brazen violation of United Nations agreements and resolutions?

Ford and Kissinger have the inveterate habit of using blackmail and threat as a tool of foreign policy. Not long ago they threatened the oil-producing countries with military measures. Now they are using the same cynical and shameless language against Cuba. They are not the first Yankee rulers who have used, to no avail, these intimidating tactics against our homeland. Eisenhower, Kennedy, Johnson, and Nixon all tried to intimidate Cuba. All, without exception, underestimated the Cuban Revolution; all were mistaken. [*Applause*] Cuba cannot be intimidated by bellicose threats. It is possible to know when and how a war on Cuba can be started; four madmen could decide that at any time; but what is impossible to know is when and how it would end. [*Prolonged applause*]

Only peoples who have no dignity can be intimidated. We have already lived through the October Crisis of 1962, and scores of atomic weapons pointed at Cuba did not make our people—not even the children—hesitate. [*Applause*] The people of Cuba can answer Kissinger's threats with the verses of a classical Spanish poem:

> *And if I fall,*
> *What is life?*
> *I already*
> *Gave it up for lost*
> *When,*
> *Without fear,*
> *I tore off the yoke*
> *Of the slave.*[7]
> [Applause]

The Yankee imperialists have hundreds of thousands of soldiers abroad; they have military bases on all continents and in all seas. In Korea, Japan, the Philippines, Turkey, Western Europe, Panama, and many other places, their military installations can be counted by the dozens and the hundreds. In Cuba itself they occupy by force a piece of our territory.

What moral and legal right do they have to protest that Cuba provides instructors and assistance for the technical preparation of the armies of African countries and of other parts of the underdeveloped world that request them?

What right do they have to criticize the aid and solidarity we give to a sister people of Africa such as Angola, who have been criminally attacked?

The imperialists are pained that Cuba, the attacked and blockaded country they tried to destroy fifteen years ago by a mercenary invasion, is today a solid and indestructible bulwark of the world revolutionary movement, whose example of bravery, dignity, and determination gives encouragement to peoples in their struggle for liberation. [*Applause*]

On the other hand, our revolutionary action is in keeping with the world balance of forces and the interest of world peace. We are not enemies of détente or of peaceful coexistence between states with different social systems based on strict respect for the norms of international law. We would even be willing to maintain normal relations with the United States on the basis of mutual respect and sovereign equality, without renouncing any of our principles and without giving up the struggle on an international level to ensure that the norms of peaceful coexistence and respect for the rights of each nation are applied to all the peoples of the world, without exception.

The United States occupies a piece of our territory in Guantánamo; the United States has maintained a criminal blockade against our country for more than fifteen years. Cuba will never bow before this imperialist policy of hostility and force and will struggle against it tirelessly. We have said that there can be no negotiations while there is a blockade. No one can negotiate with a dagger at his chest.

It doesn't matter if we spend a further twenty years without relations with the United States. [*Applause*] We have learned to live without them, and by basing ourselves on our solid and indestructible friendship with the USSR we have advanced more in these years [*Applause*] than any other country in Latin America. While trade with the United States might perhaps mean certain advantages and a faster rate of development, we prefer to move less rapidly but with our heads held high and the flag of dignity fully unfurled. [*Prolonged applause*]

We will not sell the revolutionary birthright we hold as the first socialist revolution in the Western Hemisphere for a mess of pottage. [*Applause*]

---

7. From "The Pirate's Song" by José de Espronceda (1808–42).

WE STAKED EVERYTHING IN ANGOLA

Fidel Castro
DECEMBER 1988

The victory of Cuban and Angolan forces in the four-month battle at Cuito Cuanavale (November 1987–March 1988) forced South Africa to retreat from Angola and, as Fidel Castro put it, "broke the teeth" of the South African army. His account, excerpted here, was presented to a rally of half a million people in Havana December 5, 1988.

… I believe that in the last twelve months, in the last year, our country has written one of the bravest and most extraordinary chapters of internationalism.

It all started less than thirteen months ago when the crisis developed in the People's Republic of Angola. It was a really difficult time; it was a particularly difficult situation for various reasons. We had been fulfilling our internationalist mission in that sister country for about twelve years. During those years in which we maintained our presence in Angola, we were true to our commitments not to participate in the internal strife, since each country must solve its own internal problems. Our presence was to serve as a shield against the South African threat, which is what originated our presence in Angola in 1975, at the request of that country's leadership.

On one occasion we had already driven the South Africans back to the border; that was in 1976. That year we had accumulated a large number of troops that we subsequently started to withdraw. When about half the forces we had built up in 1976 had been withdrawn, the intervention of racist and fascist South Africa started up in Angola again.

In the southern part of the country we defended a strategic line established in accord with the topography of the region and the communications required for defense. This line extended from the sea due east; first it was about three hundred kilometers long and then about seven hundred—we would have to determine the exact figure—but it extended eastward from Namibe on the coast to Menongue, in the interior of the country. We were about two hundred fifty kilometers north of the border with Namibia, and the South Africans operated without ever reaching our lines; they operated in the area between our lines and the border. Their main activity involved waging the dirty war against Angola, arming counterrevolutionary groups in association with the United States.

This situation lasted for years, but during all that time the relationship of forces favored the South Africans. Our forces were sufficient to defend that line but not to prevent South African incursions in part of Angolan territory. As I said, that situation lasted for years, until 1987, when the crisis I mentioned came about.

The crisis stemmed from an offensive organized by the People's Armed Forces for the Liberation of Angola (FAPLA) against UNITA in southeast Angola, very far from the eastern end of our lines. The Cubans were never involved in that offensive. This wasn't the first offensive; there had been another in 1985 from a point now known as Cuito Cuanavale.

Cuito Cuanavale was two hundred kilometers east of the endpoint of the Cuban line, two hundred kilometers from Menongue. It was where the 1985 FAPLA offensive against UNITA began toward the southeast. When they had advanced about one hundred fifty kilometers in that remote

---

This speech appears in full in Fidel Castro, *In Defense of Socialism: Four Speeches on the 30th Anniversary of the Cuban Revolution* (Pathfinder, 1989).

region, the South African forces intervened, very far from our lines, three hundred fifty kilometers from the endpoint of our lines, forcing the FAPLA to fall back.

To tell the truth, we had our own viewpoints about those operations, and one of our views was that these types of offensives could not be undertaken without making allowances for South African intervention. We had very clear, very precise, and very categorical views on the issue.

There were no such offensives in 1986.

Our view was that if the aim was to take the offensive along these lines inside Angola—which is an undeniable right of the Angolan government—the appropriate conditions had to be brought about to prevent South Africa from intervening. The appropriate conditions had to be brought about to prevent South African intervention! We expressed our view to those who were advising such operations.

Our views were heeded in 1986, but unfortunately they were not heeded sufficiently in 1987 and events unfolded just as we expected. At a given moment in those remote areas of eastern Angola, when the FAPLA offensive was successfully under way against UNITA, the South Africans again intervened with artillery, tanks, planes, and troops.

But in 1987 they did not limit themselves to intervening to stop the FAPLA. As had happened in 1985, this 1987 intervention occurred north of Mavinga. Mavinga is so far away that not even our fighter planes based in Menongue could reach it. As I was saying, this time the South Africans did not limit themselves to repelling the offensive. Instead they advanced toward Cuito Cuanavale in pursuit of the FAPLA and tried to destroy the largest and best group of Angolan troops. Cuito Cuanavale, as I said, is two hundred kilometers east of Menongue, the eastern end of our lines. There the South Africans tried to decide the war against Angola in their and UNITA's favor.

Of course that faraway spot was not the ideal place for large battles since logistics and organizing supplies were very difficult. To get from Menongue to Cuito Cuanavale, you had to cover two hundred kilometers through the jungle. In other words, the enemy had selected the field of battle that best suited it.

Once that situation had been created—a situation that in truth developed because our military views were not taken into account, a difficult situation that could prove to be decisive—then everybody asked us to act and try to avoid a disaster there. Everybody asked us to act and expected Cuba to solve the problem.

But actually, as we saw it, the Cuban forces and equipment in Angola were not sufficient to solve the problem. We didn't have enough men and equipment to defend a line more than seven hundred kilometers long and, what's more, to advance two hundred kilometers eastward through the jungle to deal with the problem. We ran the risk of becoming strong there and weak elsewhere, the risk of falling into a giant trap.

Therefore, from the start we saw the situation clearly. We concluded that although the problem could be solved, it was indispensable to reinforce the troops and apply an appropriate military conception. The principle was that you should not undertake decisive battles on terrain chosen by the enemy; you must wage decisive battles when you choose the terrain and strike the enemy in sensitive and genuinely strategic spots.

The crisis situation developed in mid-November. I had just returned from the Soviet Union where I had attended the festivities surrounding the seventieth anniversary of the October revolution. A few days after I got back, the news from Angola started coming in. The situation had become critical, the South Africans were on the outskirts of Cuito Cuanavale, the threat was serious, and there wasn't a minute to lose.

It was on November 15, 1987, when we met with the general staff of our Revolutionary Armed Forces and made the political and military decision to deal with the situation and take the necessary measures. To have done otherwise would probably have resulted in the annihilation of the best group of Angolan troops, with unforeseeable consequences for the survival of the People's Republic of Angola, as well as a complicated situation for our own forces. Therefore, after careful consideration, our party's leadership made the decision to reinforce the troops and help solve the serious problem.

But it wasn't so simple, it wasn't all so simple. There was a complex political situation. Comrade Gorbachev was to meet with President Reagan in

Washington on December 7 to discuss important issues related to world peace.[1] The action could be considered inappropriate. It was the worst possible time for a decision of this kind. The question was, either we make the decision or we face the consequences of letting the South Africans operate with impunity and decide the struggle in Angola militarily.

---

1. Mikhail Gorbachev, general secretary of the Communist Party of the Soviet Union, arrived in the United States December 7, 1987, for meetings with President Ronald Reagan. During that summit they signed a treaty to reduce intermediate-range nuclear forces.

Angola, November 1987–April 1988

Arrows denote movement of Cuban-Angolan-SWAPO forces
Cuban troop positions, November 1987
Forward position of Cuban-Angolan-SWAPO troops, April 1988

Adapted from *Granma*

In all truth, the leadership of our party and the leadership of our Revolutionary Armed Forces never hesitated for even an instant. The correct decision was made on November 15, 1987, to be exact. The first thing we did was to send to Angola the most experienced pilots in our air force, to begin aerial actions from the base at Menongue against the South African forces besieging Cuito Cuanavale. Meanwhile, we selected and began sending from Cuba the combat units and necessary weapons to meet the situation and foil the enemy plans.

The air force had a certain effect, but it wasn't enough. We had to fly in a group of advisers, officers, and cadres to Cuito Cuanavale, plus artillerymen, tank crews, and operators of arms and equipment. About two hundred in all were sent in to provide support for the Angolans, chiefly technical and advisory support. But that wasn't enough, and by land we had to send tank, artillery, and armored infantry units from two hundred kilometers away. We had to safeguard Cuito Cuanavale and prevent the enemy from wiping out the Angolan forces and capturing the town, which was becoming a symbol of resistance and of the success or failure of South Africa.

That is how the battle unfolded— and I've only mentioned part of it. We weren't trying to make it a decisive battle. Next to Cuito Cuanavale, which is a municipal seat, flows the Cuito River. There was a bridge over it and the enemy, using sophisticated methods and pilotless planes, was finally able to make it impassable. So one part of the Angolan forces was on the other side of the river, without the bridge, and the other part was to the west, where the town of Cuito Cuanavale is located.

It was a complex situation but not unsolvable. The enemy advance had to be stopped without giving them the chance to wage a decisive battle there. The enemy had to be stopped; they couldn't be allowed to destroy the group of Angolan troops and capture Cuito Cuanavale.

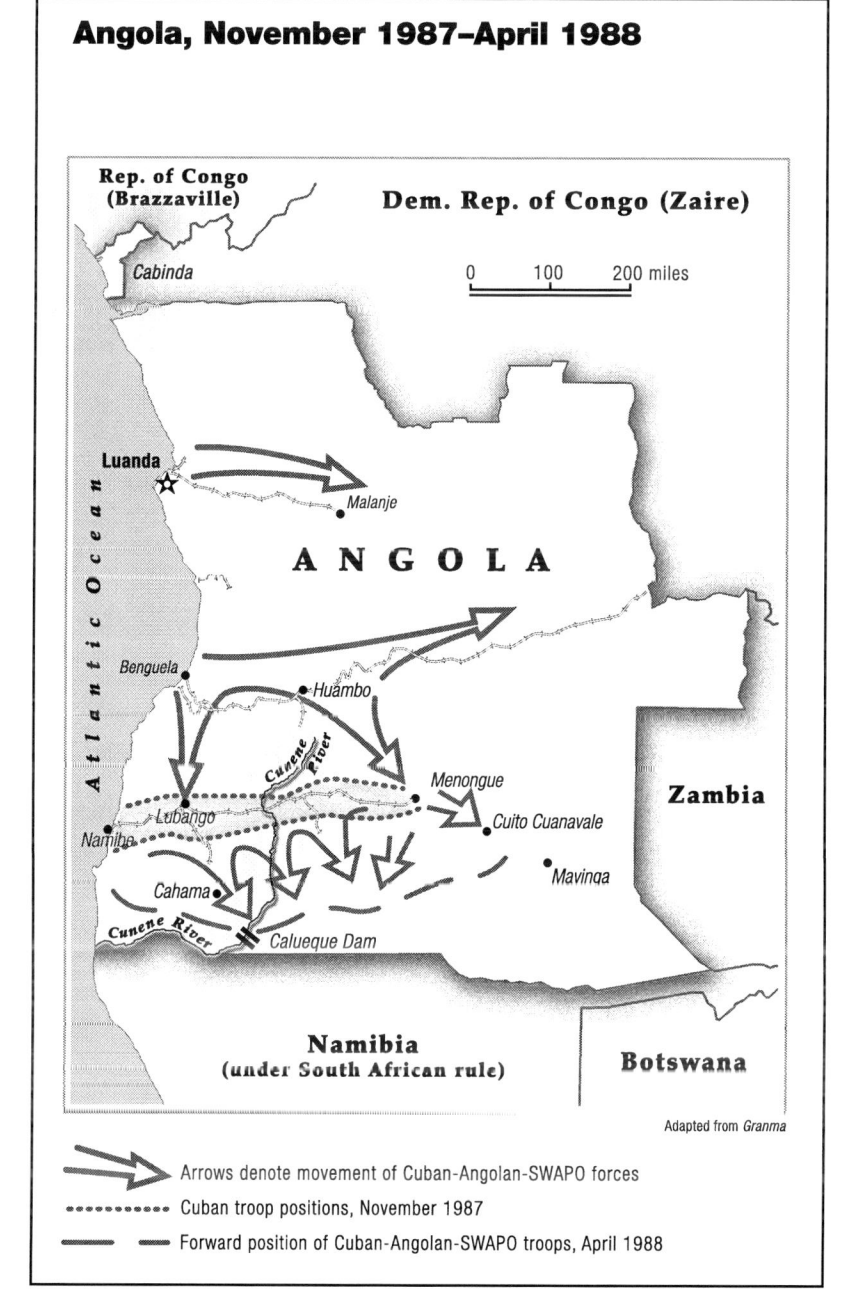

"For Cuito Cuanavale, a truly powerful force was brought together. Air, antiaircraft, and land superiority was ours.... We did not give the enemy a single opportunity!"

—*Fidel Castro, December 1988*

Top: Cuban combat pilots of MIG-23 planes (from left) Alberto Rafael Ley, Humberto Trujillo, and Antonio Rojas. **Inset:** Wreckage of South African French-made Mirage F-1 shot down by Cuban-Angolan antiaircraft batteries near Menongue, February 1988. **Above, left:** Angolan and Cuban troops unload artillery from Soviet-made IL-86 cargo plane, part of Menongue-Cuito Cuanavale supply line. **Right:** Logistical caravan heading to Cuito Cuanavale.

A more detailed explanation will have to await another occasion and different circumstances; perhaps it will be a task for writers and historians to give an explanation of exactly what happened there and how the events unfolded.

The Angolan government had assigned us the responsibility of defending Cuito Cuanavale, and all the necessary measures were taken not only to stop the South Africans but to turn Cuito Cuanavale into a trap, a trap the South African troops ran right into.

In Cuito Cuanavale the South Africans really broke their teeth and it all came about with a minimum of casualties—a minimum of casualties!—for our own forces, the Angolan and Cuban forces.

The South Africans were set on carrying out the action and they completely failed. But the Cuban-Angolan strategy wasn't simply to stop the enemy at Cuito Cuanavale, but to gather enough forces and equipment on the western end of our lines to advance southward and threaten key positions of the South African forces.

The main idea was to stop them at Cuito Cuanavale *and* deal them blows from the southwest. Enough troops were gathered together to seriously threaten points of strategic importance for South Africa and strike hard at them on terrain that we, and not the enemy, had chosen. [*Applause*]

Our troops advanced southward from the west, with enough men and equipment to fulfill their mission. It took only a few clashes with their scouting patrols and powerful air strikes at their positions in Calueque for the South Africans to realize the tremendous force they were up against, and this change in the relationship of forces was what paved the way for negotiations. No one should think that they came about by chance.

The United States had been meeting with Angola for some time, presenting themselves as mediators between the Angolans and the South Africans to seek a peaceful solution, and so the years went by. But while these supposed negotiations were taking place with the United States as intermediary, the South Africans had intervened and tried to solve the Angolan situation militarily, and perhaps they would have achieved it if not for the effort our country made.

The fact is that the relationship of forces changed radically. The South Africans suffered a crushing defeat in Cuito Cuanavale and the worst part for them was still to come. The truth is they started to play with fire and they got burned. [*Applause*]

Perhaps never in these more than twelve years had they faced so much danger. When we reached the border of Namibia in 1976 we had men, we had a good number of tanks and cannons, but we had no air force or antiaircraft missiles and we lacked much of the equipment we have today.

I must say that our pilots covered themselves with glory in the battle of Cuito Cuanavale and wrote truly extraordinary pages in history. [*Applause*] A handful of pilots went on hundreds upon hundreds of missions in only a few weeks. They had control of the air with the MiG-23s and we must say they carried out a great feat. That was an important factor.

We not only sent our best pilots to Angola, we also sent our best antiaircraft weapons, a large amount of portable antiaircraft equipment, a good quantity of antiaircraft missile artillery. We reinforced our air power and we sent as many tanks, armored troop carriers, and artillery pieces as were needed.

I mentioned the pilots, but it would also be fair to mention our tank crews' conduct, our artillerymen's conduct, that of our antiaircraft defense personnel, our infantry, our scouts, our sappers.

Village of Cuito Cuanavale in southern Angola, site of crushing defeat of South African forces in March 1988.

"At Cuito Cuanavale the South Africans really broke their teeth."
—*Fidel Castro, December 1988*

GRANMA

Top: Cuban division general Leopoldo Cintra Frías, commander of Cuban-Angolan forces on southern front, inspects South African Olifant tank captured during combat near Cuito Cuanavale, March 23, 1988.

Middle: After defeat at Cuito Cuanavale, South African government sued for peace. In photo, signing of accords at United Nations in New York, December 1988, ending the war and recognizing Namibia's independence. At table, left to right: South African defense minister Magnus Malan and foreign minister Pik Botha; UN secretary-general Javier Pérez de Cuéllar; US secretary of state George Shultz; Angolan foreign minister Alfonso Van Dunem and ambassador to US Antonio dos Santos Franca; Cuban foreign minister Isidoro Malmierca and General Abelardo Colomé.

Below: Namibians celebrate tripartite accords recognizing Namibian independence, 1988.

[*Applause*] They organized and helped set up impassable mine fields where the South African tanks were blown up in Cuito Cuanavale. [*Applause*] Success was the result of the coordinated action of the different forces there, in close cooperation with the Angolan troops who really acted with extraordinary heroism and great efficiency in the common effort.

The Angolan 25th Infantry Brigade in particular distinguished itself in the battles waged east of the river. It was a common struggle with common merit and common glory. [*Applause*]

In Cuito Cuanavale the greater part of the troops were Angolan; and in our southward advance, which we also undertook in common, the greater part of the troops were Cuban. [*Applause*]

A truly powerful force was brought together. Air, antiaircraft, and land superiority was ours. We took great care to provide air cover for our troops and so, even when the South African planes vanished from the sky after receiving a few good lessons from our antiaircraft weapons, the troops always advanced and took up their positions with a maximum of antiaircraft support. And our antiaircraft weapons were and still are on maximum alert to prevent surprise attacks. We had thoroughly analyzed the experiences of recent wars and we did not give the enemy a single opportunity, not a single opportunity! [*Applause*]

This was not just because of the measures we took on land—fortifying the field, the antiaircraft weapons, the planes—but we also performed construction feats. In a matter of weeks an airport was built for our fighters, an air base that enabled our planes to advance more than two hundred kilometers and seriously threaten the nerve centers of the South African troops. There was no improvisation, no adventure, no carelessness on our part. The enemy realized not just that they were up against very powerful forces but also highly experienced ones.

In this way the conditions were created that made possible the negotiations that have continued and have even progressed over the past few months. A radical change in the political, diplomatic, and military situation was brought about.

In these negotiations the United States has acted as mediator. You can say "mediator" in quotes, but this doesn't deprive its diplomatic action in these negotiations of a certain positive aspect. I say "mediator" in quotes because they are the allies of UNITA and provide weapons to UNITA; by doing that they act as the allies of South Africa. But at the same time they're interested in seeking a solution to the Namibian problem, seeking some peace formula for the region as a consequence of which the Cuban troops will be withdrawn from Angola.

We know that the United States had some sleepless nights over the kind of boldness whereby a small, blockaded and threatened country like Cuba was capable of carrying out an internationalist mission of this nature. The empire can't conceive of this. They are the only ones in the world who are entitled to have troops everywhere, weapons everywhere, bases everywhere. And so the fact that a small Caribbean country was capable of providing support to a sister African nation is something beyond their parameters, concepts, and norms.

It's clear that this internationalist mission carried out by Cuba had a very big impact on Africa. The African peoples, and even African governments that are not revolutionary but belong rather to the right have viewed with admiration the mission carried out by Cuba in Africa. The African peoples know these are troops allied with them; they know that the only non-African country whose troops were sent to defend an African country against the aggression of racist and fascist South Africa is Cuba. [*Applause*]

All of Africa deeply hates apartheid. All of Africa views apartheid as their greatest enemy, an enemy that despises Africa, attacks Africa, humiliates Africa. It's incredible up to what point the African peoples suffer from apartheid, and this has turned African feelings, the African soul, into an ally of Cuba.

The imperialists can't understand very well the reason for Cuba's broad relations on the international scene, Cuba's prestige on the international scene. But the African peoples, who have been so humiliated by apartheid and racism, have been able to appraise in all its dimensions the noble, generous gesture, the historical dimension, the heroism of our people who were capable not only of defending themselves here from such a powerful enemy but also help the Africans in their struggle against the fascists and racists.

We know what the African peoples think—and this is another problem hanging over US policy. The

African peoples have viewed the United States as an ally and friend of apartheid and see it as mainly to blame for apartheid's survival. And South Africa has become an embarrassing friend for the United States. Apartheid has become something that is politically negative for US standing before world public opinion, something that stinks in US policy. It is something that even causes it domestic problems, because there are sectors in the United States that condemn apartheid, repudiate apartheid, criticize apartheid. These include the black population in the United States, and not just the black population but the minorities who suffer discrimination in the United States, and not just national minorities but also a large portion of US public opinion.

And so apartheid and its alliance with the US government are becoming an internal political problem, hence the US interest in steering clear of it, of making people stop thinking it is associated with or an ally of apartheid.

Similarly the problem of Namibia, occupied by South Africa, is a problem that concerns world public opinion as a whole. It concerns the United Nations. Long ago the United Nations ordered the South Africans to leave Namibia and many years ago the UN adopted Resolution 435 on Namibia's independence.[2]

Thus the United States could kill three birds with one stone: distance itself more from apartheid to improve its relations with Africa; make an effort to have UN Resolution 435 applied; and finally, what deprives them of so much sleep, obtain the withdrawal of Cuban troops from Angola. These are the objectives the United States has pursued: improving its international image, improving its image in the eyes of the African peoples, making some advance to place themselves in a more comfortable position before world public opinion, and having the Cuban troops withdraw from Angola.

The truth is that Cuba has no economic interest in Angola or in Africa. Cuba has no strategic interest in Angola or in Africa nor can it, because Cuba is not a big power but a small country. Cuba is in Angola by virtue of internationalist principles, by virtue of its feelings of solidarity, because it is doing its duty of helping other peoples. It is doing its

---

2. See glossary, UN Security Council Resolution 435.

"As we have said before, being internationalists is paying our debt to humanity," said Fidel Castro in December 1988. "Those who are incapable of fighting for others will never be capable of fighting for themselves." **Above:** Combined Cuban and MPLA forces receive orientation during "Operation Menongue" in southern Angola, February–March 1978.

duty of helping the African peoples against apartheid, against racism, against colonialism, against foreign aggression. No other country is more interested than Cuba in bringing its troops back; no one is more interested in this than Cuba. No one benefits more than Cuba, no one is more desirous of bringing the troops back than Cuba. . . .

A large portion of our leadership's time, of my time, of the Revolutionary Armed Forces' time, was taken up with [the Angolan mission] throughout the year. I already told you it wasn't easy making that decision and, above all, I mentioned the moment when the decision was taken. I already told you in essence that it was on the eve of the Gorbachev-Reagan meeting. There were some who came to believe we were plotting against peace, plotting against détente, given the circumstances under which we felt compelled to send the reinforcements. But given the situation I assure you we couldn't have lost a single day, we couldn't have lost a single minute. One minute lost and it would have been too late.

There are moments when difficult and bitter decisions have to be taken, and when that moment came our party and our armed forces did not hesitate for an instant. I believe that helped prevent a political calamity, a military calamity for Angola, for Africa, and for all progressive forces. I believe that decisively boosted the prospects for peace now present in the region.

I believe that on a day like today tribute should be paid to the efforts made by our troops and by our people. This is a mission we can all feel proud of; it is one more page of glory for our fighting people, our armed forces, born on October 10, 1868, and reborn on December 2, 1956.[3] [*Applause*]

There are some who have even dared question the internationalist spirit and heroism of our people, who have criticized it. This is the Yankees' hope: that anti-internationalist currents would arise among our people to weaken us. As we have said before, being internationalists is paying our debt to humanity. [*Applause*] Those who are incapable of fighting for others will never be capable of fighting for themselves. [*Applause*] And the heroism shown by our forces, by our people in other lands, faraway lands, must also serve to let the imperialists know what awaits them if one day they force us to fight on this land here. [*Applause and shouts*]. . . .

---

3. The first war for Cuban independence opened October 10, 1868. On December 2, 1956, the *Granma* expeditionaries landed in eastern Cuba, opening the revolutionary war against the US-backed Batista dictatorship.

ALL WE TAKE WITH US FROM AFRICA ARE THE REMAINS OF OUR COMBATANTS WHO DIED FIGHTING FOR FREEDOM

Fidel Castro
DECEMBER 1989

Speech by Fidel Castro at ceremony in Havana, December 7, 1989, honoring the more than 2,000 Cuban volunteers killed in internationalist missions around the world. The great majority of these combatants had fallen during the mission in Angola, begun fourteen years earlier.

Comrade president Jose Eduardo dos Santos and other guests,
Relatives of our fallen comrades,
Combatants,
Fellow countrymen:

December 7, the memorable date on which Antonio Maceo, the most illustrious of our soldiers, and his young aide-de-camp were killed in combat, has always been a day of great significance for all Cubans. Their remains lie here in this sacred corner of the motherland. By choosing this day to bury the remains of our heroic internationalist fighters who have died in different parts of the world—mainly in Africa, where Maceo's ancestors and much of our blood came from—we make it a day for honoring all Cubans who gave their lives while defending their country and all of mankind. Patriotism and internationalism—two of man's most treasured values—are joined together forever in Cuba's history.

Perhaps someday a monument will be built not far from this site to honor them.

At this very moment, the remains of the internationalists who died carrying out their noble and glorious mission are being laid to rest simultaneously in their hometowns all over Cuba.

The imperialist enemy thought we would conceal the number of our casualties in Angola—the longest and most complex mission, which has already reached fourteen years—as if it were a dishonor or a discredit for the revolution. For a long time they dreamed that the blood that had been shed would be in vain, as if the death of someone who dies for a just cause could be in vain. Even if the value of the sacrifices made by mankind in their just struggles could only be gauged by the crude measuring stick of victory, we should note that they did return with a victory.

The Spartans used to say you return with your shield or on your shield. Our troops returned with their shields.

It is not my intention on this solemn occasion to boast of our achievements or to humiliate anyone, not even those who were our adversaries. Our country sought neither glory nor military prestige. We always followed rigorously the principle of reaching our objective with the smallest sacrifice of lives possible. To do this, we had to be strong, act calmly, and as we always did, be willing to do anything.

Every combatant knew that the whole country was behind him. They knew that we were all concerned about their health and safety.

When it became possible to use political and diplomatic efforts to attain the final goals, we did not hesitate for a moment to use those channels. We always acted with the necessary firmness, yet at no time during the negotiation process did you see any arrogance, high-handedness, or bragging from us. We were flexible whenever flexibility was advisable and fair.

The final stage of the war in Angola was the most difficult. It demanded our country's determination, tenacity, and fighting spirit in support of our Angolan brothers.

From the December 18, 1989, issue of *Granma Weekly Review*.

In fulfilling this duty of solidarity, not only to Angola but also to our own combatants fighting under difficult conditions there, the revolution did not hesitate to stake everything. Even when the imperialist threats against our own country were enormous, we didn't hesitate in sending much of our most modern and best military equipment to the Southern Front of the People's Republic of Angola. Over fifty thousand Cuban combatants went to that sister nation at that time, a truly impressive figure if you take into account the distance they had to travel and our country's size and resources. It was a veritable feat by our Revolutionary Armed Forces and our people. Such chapters of selflessness and international solidarity are seldom seen in history.

That's why we appreciate very much the presence of Jose Eduardo dos Santos in this ceremony. It was an entirely spontaneous gesture: "I want to be with you on this occasion," he said. The leaders of Ethiopia, the South West Africa People's Organisation, and of other countries and revolutionary organizations, as soon as they learned about this ceremony just a few days ago, also spontaneously said that they too wanted to send representatives to be here with us today when we laid to rest all of our internationalists who died in Africa and in other countries.

There are historic events that nothing and no one can erase. There are revolutionary examples that the best men and women of future generations, both inside and outside our country, will never forget. This is one of them, yet we should not be the ones to judge it; history will do so.

We cannot forget for a moment that our comrades-in-arms were the heroic combatants of the Angolan armed forces. Tens of thousands of the best sons and daughters of that extraordinary people gave their lives. Victory was possible because of the closest unity and cooperation between them and us.

We also had the honor of fighting alongside the courageous sons and daughters of Namibia, the patriots of Guinea-Bissau, and the unmatched soldiers of Ethiopia. Years earlier, during the difficult period immediately following Algeria's independence,[1] our internationalist fighters were at their side. Later they were also in Syria, another sister Arab nation that was a victim of foreign aggression and requested our cooperation.[2]

There is no just cause in Africa that has not received our people's support. Che Guevara and a large group of Cuban revolutionaries fought white mercenaries in the eastern part of what is now Zaire, and today doctors and teachers are working generously and selflessly in the Western Sahara republic, helping its people, who are fighting for their freedom.

All of these countries were independent at the time or are now independent. Those that have not yet won their independence will do so, sooner or later.

In just a few years, our fighters wrote an exemplary chapter of solidarity, one that our people can be proud of. Men from other countries also fought at our side in our own struggles for independence. Máximo Gómez, who was born in the Dominican Republic, became the chief of our Liberation Army because of his extraordinary merits. In the years prior to our revolution, one thousand Cubans organized by the first Communist Party fought in Spain to defend the republic. They wrote memorable chapters of heroism, which Pablo de la Torriente Brau recorded for the pages of history until death put an early end to the life of that brilliant revolutionary journalist.

That was how our internationalist spirit was forged, and it reached its zenith with the socialist revolution.

Wherever Cuban internationalists have gone, they have set examples of respect for the dignity and sovereignty of those countries. The trust that those peoples have placed in them is not by chance; it's the result of their irreproachable behavior. That's why our exemplary selflessness and concern for others is remembered everywhere.

A prominent African leader once said in a meeting of leaders of the region, "Cuban combatants are ready to give their lives for the liberation of our countries. The only thing they will take from us in exchange for that help for our freedom and our peoples' progress are the bodies of those who died

---

1. Troops of the Moroccan monarchy, with backing from Paris and other imperialist powers, invaded eastern Algeria in late September 1963, a little more than a year after the Algerian people had won independence from France. At the request of the new Algerian government for aid, revolutionary Cuba sent 686 combatants, including a tank battalion and an artillery group. The Moroccan assault was defeated and a cease-fire was signed at the end of October.

2. See footnote, p. 29.

fighting for freedom."[3] A continent that had experienced centuries of exploitation and plunder could appreciate the full extent of the selflessness of our internationalist contribution.

Now, our battle-seasoned combatants are returning victoriously. The joyful, happy, proud faces of mothers, wives, brothers, sisters, sons, and daughters—of all our people—welcome them with warmth and emotion. Peace was achieved with honor, and the fruit of their sacrifices and efforts have by far exceeded expectations. Our sleep is no longer disturbed by the constant concern over the fate of our soldiers fighting thousands of kilometers from their land.

The enemy thought that our troops' return would cause social problems, that it would be impossible to provide jobs for them all. Most of those men—in addition to the cadres from the armed forces—had work here in Cuba and will go back to their old jobs or to better ones. Not one of them has been forgotten. Many already knew where they would be working even before they returned.

None of the young men in military service who shortly after graduating from high school volunteered for the honor of being part of the internationalist mission in Angola have had to wait to occupy a worthy place in the classrooms or among our workers.

Our country is working hard to carry out ambitious programs for social and economic development. We are not guided by the irrational laws of capitalism. Every son and daughter of our country has a job in education, production, or in services.

No close relatives of those who died fulfilling their mission or who suffered serious injuries have been forgotten. They have received, are receiving, and will continue to receive all the care and consideration due to them for the noble sacrifices made by their loved ones and for their own self-sacrificing, selfless, generous, and even heroic behavior.

The hundreds of thousands of Cubans who car-

On December 7, 1989, in each municipality, Cubans paid homage to the 2,077 combatants who fell serving internationalist missions in Africa. They were interred in their home towns. "All we take with us from Africa are the remains of those who died fighting for freedom," said Fidel Castro at the ceremony in Havana. **Above:** Interment ceremony in Artemisa, near Havana, December 1989.

ried out military or civilian internationalist missions will always have the respect of present and future generations. They multiplied many times the glorious fighting and internationalist traditions of our people.

The country they found upon their return is engaged in a colossal struggle for development while continuing to confront the criminal imperialist blockade with exemplary dignity. In addition we face the crisis that has emerged in the socialist camp, from which our country can only expect negative economic consequences.[4]

In most of those socialist countries they aren't talking about the struggle against imperialism or the principles of internationalism. Those words aren't even mentioned in their press. Such concepts have virtually been removed from political dictionaries there. Meanwhile capitalist values are gaining unusual strength in those societies.

Capitalism means unequal terms of trade with the peoples of the Third World; the exacerbation of individual selfishness and national chauvinism;

---

3. The words of Amilcar Cabral, leader of the independence struggle in Guinea-Bissau and Cape Verde.

4. The Berlin Wall fell on November 9, 1989, two days after this speech. The subsequent disintegration of the Soviet Union and cancelation of trade and aid agreements led to a severe economic crisis in Cuba known as the Special Period.

the reign of irrationality and anarchy in investment and production; the ruthless sacrifice of the peoples under blind economic laws; the rule of the stronger; the exploitation of men by men; a situation of everyone for himself. In the social sphere, capitalism implies many more things: prostitution; drugs; gambling; begging; unemployment; abysmal inequalities among citizens; the depletion of natural resources; the poisoning of the air, seas, rivers, and forests; and especially the plundering of the underdeveloped nations by the industrialized capitalist countries. In the past, it meant colonialism. Now it means the neocolonization of billions of human beings through more sophisticated economic and political methods—methods that are cheaper, more effective, and more ruthless.

Capitalism's market economy, its values, categories, and methods can never be the tools to pull socialism out of its present difficulties, or to rectify whatever mistakes have been made. Most of those difficulties are the result not just of errors, but also of the harsh blockade and isolation imposed on the socialist countries by imperialism and the major capitalist powers. They monopolize nearly all the world's wealth and most advanced technologies, which they accomplished by plundering the colonies, exploiting the working class, and conducting a massive brain drain from countries that were on the verge of developing.

Devastating wars were unleashed against the first socialist state, taking a toll of millions of lives and destroying most of the means of production that had been created. Like a phoenix, the first socialist state had to rise more than once from its ashes. It performed great services to mankind by defeating fascism and decisively supporting the liberation movements in countries still under colonial rule. Now, they want to forget all of this.

It's repugnant to see how many people, even in the USSR itself, are engaged in denying and destroying the great historic feats and extraordinary merits of that heroic people. That is not the way to rectify and overcome the undeniable errors made in a revolution that emerged from tsarist authoritarianism in a huge, backward, and poor country. We shouldn't blame Lenin now for having made the greatest revolution in history in the old Russia of the tsars.

This is why we haven't hesitated to stop the circulation of certain Soviet publications that are full of poison against the USSR itself and against socialism. You can see that imperialism, reactionary forces, and the counterrevolution are behind them. Some of those publications have already begun calling for an end to the fair and equitable trade relations that were established between the USSR and Cuba during the Cuban revolutionary process. In short, they want the USSR to begin having unequal trade with Cuba by selling us their products at increasingly higher prices and buying our agricultural goods and raw materials at lower and lower prices. They want them to act the same way the United States does with Third World countries—ultimately, they want the USSR to be part of the US blockade against Cuba.

Imperialism's systematic undermining and destruction of the values of socialism, combined with the mistakes that have been made, has accelerated the process of destabilization in the socialist countries in Eastern Europe. Differentiated treatment for each country while undermining socialism from within—that was the long-term strategy created and implemented by the United States.

Imperialism and the capitalist powers cannot hide their glee over what's happening. They are convinced—not without reason—that, at this point, the socialist camp has virtually ceased to exist. Groups of US citizens, including US presidential advisers, are planning capitalist development in some of those Eastern European countries right now. A recent news dispatch reported that they were fascinated by that "exciting experience." One of them, a US government official, was in favor of implementing in Poland a program similar to the New Deal, with which Roosevelt tried to alleviate the great crisis of capitalism. This would be to help the 600,000 Polish workers who will lose their jobs in 1990 and half of the 17.8 million workers in the country's workforce who will have to be retrained and change jobs as a result of the implementation of a market economy.

Imperialism and the NATO capitalist powers are convinced—not without reason—that at this point the Warsaw Pact does not exist either, that it is nothing more than a fiction. And that societies that were corroded and undermined from within will not be able to resist.

It has been stated that socialism must be improved. No one can be opposed to this principle, which is inherently and permanently applicable to every human endeavor. But can socialism be improved by forsaking the most basic principles of Marxism and Leninism? Why must the so-called reforms go toward capitalism? If those ideas are truly revolutionary, as some claim, why do they receive the imperialist leaders' unanimous, enthusiastic support?

In a very unusual statement, the president of the United States described himself as the number-one advocate of the doctrines currently being applied in many countries in the socialist camp.

In history there has never been a truly revolutionary idea that has received the enthusiastic support of the leader of the most powerful, aggressive, and voracious empire known to mankind.

Following comrade Gorbachev's visit to Cuba in April this year—a visit during which we had a deep and frank exchange of views—we publicly expressed in the National Assembly our view that the right of any socialist country to build capitalism, if that's their wish, should be respected. Just as we demand complete respect for the right of any capitalist country to build socialism.

We believe that revolution cannot be imported or exported; a socialist state cannot be founded through artificial insemination or by means of an embryo transplant. A revolution requires appropriate conditions within a society, and only each individual people can create them. These ideas don't run counter to the solidarity that revolutionaries can and should extend to one another. Moreover, a revolution is a process that may advance or regress, a process that may even fail. But above all, communists must be courageous and revolutionary. Communists are duty-bound to struggle under all circumstances, no matter how adverse they may be. The Paris communards fought and died in the defense of their ideas. The banners of the revolution and of socialism are not surrendered without a fight. Only cowards and the demoralized surrender—it's unbecoming of communists and other revolutionaries.

Now imperialism is urging the socialist countries in Europe to accept its surplus capital, to develop capitalism, and to join in plundering the Third World countries.

It's a well-known fact that a large part of the wealth of the developed capitalist world comes from unequal trade with these countries. For centuries, those nations were plundered as colonies. Millions of their sons and daughters were enslaved. In many instances their silver and other mineral resources were exhausted. They were pitilessly exploited and underdevelopment was imposed upon them. Underdevelopment was the most direct and clearest consequence of the period of colonial rule. Today they're exploited through payment of interest on endless unpayable debt. Their basic commodities are extracted at ridiculously low prices. And they're forced to pay ever higher prices for the industrial goods they import. Financial and human resources are constantly being drawn from those nations through the flight of capital and the brain drain. Their trade is blocked through "dumping," high tariffs, import quotas, synthetic substitutes produced through advanced technological processes, and subsidizing production in the developed countries when they aren't competitive.

Imperialism wants the socialist countries in Europe to join in this colossal plunder—an invitation which seems not to displease the theoreticians of capitalist reforms. Thus, in many of those countries, no one speaks about the tragedy of the Third World, and their discontented multitudes are guided toward capitalism and anticommunism—and, in one country toward Pan-Germanism. The evolution of these events may even lead to fascist trends. The prize imperialism promises them is a share of the plunder wrested from our peoples, the only way they can build capitalist consumer societies.

The United States and the other capitalist powers are much more interested in investing in Eastern Europe today than in any other part of the world. What resources can the Third World—in which billions of people live in subhuman conditions—expect from such developments?

They speak to us of peace, but what kind of peace? Of peace between the major powers, while imperialism reserves to itself the right to overtly intervene in and attack Third World countries. There are many examples of this.

The imperialist government of the United States demands that no one help the Salvadoran revolutionaries and tries to blackmail the USSR into ending its economic and military assistance to Nicaragua and Cuba because we extend solidarity to the Salvadoran revolutionaries, even though we abide strictly to our commitments regarding the weapons supplied by the USSR in accordance with the agreements signed between sovereign nations.

Meanwhile, the same imperialist government that is demanding an end to all solidarity with Salvadoran revolutionaries is helping the genocidal Salvadoran government and sending special combat units to El Salvador; supporting the counterrevolution in Nicaragua; organizing coups d'état in Panama and the assassination of leaders from that country; sending military aid to UNITA in Angola—in spite of the successful peace agreements in south western Africa; and continuing to supply the rebel forces in Afghanistan with large amounts of weapons, ignoring the Geneva accords and the fact that the Soviet troops have withdrawn.

Just a few days ago US war planes shamelessly intervened in an internal conflict in the Philippines. Regardless of whether or not the rebel forces had good cause for their action—which it is not our place to judge—US intervention in that country is a very serious matter and is an accurate reflection of the current world situation. The United States has taken upon itself the role of gendarme, not only in Latin America—a region it has always considered its own backyard—but also in any other Third World country.

The consecration of the principle of universal intervention by a major power represents an end to independence and sovereignty in the world. What kind of peace and security can our peoples have other than what we ourselves achieve through our own heroism?

Getting rid of nuclear weapons is a wonderful idea. If it were more than simply a utopia and could be achieved someday, it would be unquestionably beneficial and would increase world safety—but only for a part of humanity. It would not bring peace, safety, or hope to the Third World countries.

Imperialism doesn't need nuclear weapons to attack our peoples. Its powerful fleets spread all over the world, its military bases everywhere, and its ever more sophisticated and lethal conventional weapons are enough to ensure its role as the world's master and gendarme.

Moreover, forty thousand children who could be saved die every day in our world because of underdevelopment and poverty. As we've said before—and it's worth repeating it today—it's as if a bomb similar to the ones dropped on Hiroshima and Nagasaki were dropped every three days on the poor children in the world.

If these developments continue on their present course and the United States isn't forced to renounce these concepts, what new way of thinking can we speak of? Following this course, the bipolar world that emerged in the postwar period will inexorably become a unipolar world under US domination.

In Cuba, we are carrying out a process of rectification. It's impossible to carry out a revolution or conduct a rectification without a strong, disciplined, and respected party. It's not possible to carry out such a process by slandering socialism, destroying its values, discrediting the party, demoralizing its vanguard, abandoning its leadership role, eliminating social discipline, and sowing chaos and anarchy everywhere. This may foster a counterrevolution— but not revolutionary change.

The US imperialists think that Cuba won't be able to resist and that the new situation in the socialist camp will inexorably crush our revolution.

Cuba is not a country in which socialism came in the wake of victorious divisions of the Red Army. In Cuba, socialism was forged by Cubans through a legitimate, heroic struggle. Thirty years of resistance against the most powerful empire on earth, which tried to destroy our revolution, testifies to our political and moral strength.

Those of us in our country's leadership aren't a bunch of inexperienced outsiders, new to positions of responsibility. We come from the ranks of the school of old anti-imperialist fighters like Mella and Guiteras; from the ranks of those who attacked the Moncada and came on the *Granma*; who fought in the Sierra Maestra and the underground struggle, from Playa Girón and the October [1962 "missile"] crisis; from thirty years of heroic resistance against imperialist aggression; from the ranks of those who performed great feats of labor and took part in glorious internationalist missions. Men and women from three generations of Cubans come together and assume responsibilities in our battle-seasoned party, our marvelous vanguard youth organization, in our powerful mass organizations, in our glorious Revolutionary Armed Forces and Ministry of the Interior.

In Cuba, revolution, socialism, and national independence are inextricably united.

We owe everything we are today to the revolution and socialism. If Cuba were ever to return to capitalism, our independence and sovereignty would be lost forever. We would be an extension of Miami, a mere appendage of US imperialism. The repugnant prophecy that a US president made in the nineteenth century when they were considering the annexation of Cuba—that our island would fall into its hands like a piece of ripe fruit—would be fulfilled. There will be a people willing to give their lives to prevent this today, tomorrow, and always. It's worth repeating here, at Maceo's tomb, his immortal phrase: "Anyone who attempts to conquer Cuba shall reap only its blood-soaked soil, if he doesn't perish in the struggle first."

We Cuban communists and the millions of revolutionary combatants who are part of the ranks of our historic and combative people will carry out the role assigned to us in history, not only as the first socialist state in the western hemisphere but also as intransigent frontline defenders of the noble cause of all the destitute, exploited people of the world.

We have never aspired to receiving custody of the banners and the principles the revolutionary movement has defended throughout its heroic and inspiring history. However, if some day fate were to assigned to us the role of being among the last defenders of socialism, in a world in which US imperialism has realized Hitler's dreams of world domination, we would defend this bulwark to the last drop of our blood.

These men and women whom we are laying to rest today in the land of their birth gave their lives for the most treasured values of our history and our revolution.

They died fighting against colonialism and neocolonialism.

They died fighting against racism and apartheid.

They died fighting against the plunder and exploitation of the third world.

They died fighting for the independence and sovereignty of those peoples.

They died fighting for the right of all peoples in the world to ensure their well-being and development.

They died fighting so there would be no hungry people or beggars, sick people without doctors, children without schools; human beings without work, shelter, and food.

They died so there would be no oppressors or oppressed, no exploiters or exploited.

They died fighting for the dignity and freedom of all men and women.

They died fighting for true peace and security for all nations.

They died defending the ideals of Céspedes and Máximo Gómez.

They died defending the ideals of Martí and Maceo.

They died defending the ideals of Marx, Engels, and Lenin.

They died defending the ideals and example that the October Revolution extended throughout the world.

They died for socialism.

They died for internationalism.

They died for the proud, revolutionary homeland that Cuba is today.

We will follow their example.

Eternal glory to them.

¡Socialismo o muerte! [Socialism or death!]

¡Patria o muerte! [Homeland or death!]

¡Venceremos! [We will win!]

THANKS TO ANGOLA, WE KNOW BETTER WHAT WE ARE CAPABLE OF ACHIEVING

Raúl Castro
MAY 1991

Speech given May 27, 1991, greeting the final contingent of internationalist volunteers returning from Angola. The ceremony was held in Havana at El Cacahual, the burial site of nineteenth-century independence leader Antonio Maceo.

☙

Distinguished guests,
Internationalist combatants,
Compañeras and compañeros:

The last person to return home among the Cuban internationalist combatants who remained in the People's Republic of Angola until Saturday, May 25, was the head of the Cuban military mission in that sister nation,[1] and the undefeated combat flag of the mission, which symbolized the long and difficult road that began in 1975, is now here with us once again.

Cuba's troops, with their weapons, have withdrawn from Angola more than a month ahead of the deadline agreed upon in the December 1988 accords.

For the Cuban nation this is a time of paying tribute and a time of remembrance—a tribute of admiration, gratitude, and respect for the 377,033 sons and daughters of our people who for nearly sixteen years gave Angola their resolute collaboration in defense of its sovereignty and territorial integrity, and for the close to 50,000 other Cubans who throughout this same period expressed their solidarity by carrying out civilian tasks.

We honor here, above all, our 2,077 comrades who didn't survive to see the victory they shed their blood for. They will always be among the nation's most beloved sons and daughters. We bow our heads to their undying example. With infinite respect we evoke here today the no less exemplary conduct of their parents, children, spouses, and relatives, who gave them encouragement while they were fighting far from the land of their birth.

However, what brought us together here this morning is not just the heroic achievement of the Angolan and Cuban peoples, whose brotherhood is based on the generous blood spilled and the sweat of labor.

Angola is a landmark, a milestone in history that will continue to inspire the African peoples' desire for national independence and social emancipation. It is an eternal flame that can never be snuffed out, no matter how hard and bitter the setbacks may be.

Angola is a brilliant, clean, honorable, transparent page in the history of solidarity among peoples, in the history of internationalism, in the history of Cuba's contribution to the cause of freedom and human progress. Angola is also, because of all of that, a landmark in Cuban history as well.

The fathers of our nation would be proud of our internationalist course. Buried in this sanctuary of the nation are the remains of General Antonio Maceo, the invincible leader of the Baraguá Protest [during Cuba's war for independence in 1878], within whose veins flowed the unredeemed blood of Africa and who more than once offered to place his sword at the service of the cause of Puerto Rican independence. The titans in the Cuban *mambí* independence army didn't hesitate for one second in offering Dominican Máximo Gómez the supreme command, which he so well deserved. This was the highest expression of Latin Americanism

---

Published in Raúl Castro, ¡*La operación Carlota ha concluido! Victoria del internacionalismo cubano* [Operation Carlota is over! A victory for Cuban internationalism] (Havana: Editora Política, 1991).

"Angola is an honorable page in the history of solidarity among peoples, of internationalism, of Cuba's contribution to the cause of freedom and human progress."
—Raúl Castro, May 1991

Above: Luanda airport, May 25, 1991. Brigadier General Samuel Rodiles Planas, head of Cuban military mission in Angola, waves Cuba's flag moments after last group of combatants boards plane to return to Cuba.
Below: Arriving at Havana airport, later the same day.

and solidarity with the cause of independence of the Cuban people.

Fighting in the ranks of the Liberation Army on the battlefields in 1868 and 1895[2] were men from different latitudes, mixing together in the Cuban brush with whites and blacks native to the country and waging the same epic struggle for freedom. Among hundreds of fighters from nearly twenty countries, according to information that is not complete, at least seventeen of them rose to the rank of general.

It has been verified that this distinction was awarded to five from the Dominican Republic, three from Spain, two from the United States, two from Colombia, and one each from Chile, Jamaica, Puerto Rico, Poland, and Venezuela. Each of them in their moment contributed the commitment, moral greatness, and selflessness that helped shape our internationalist tradition.

The tradition was continued, through his exemplary conduct, by Pablo de la Torriente Brau of Puerto Rico, who became a man and a revolutionary during the Cuban struggle and later became a hero during the Spanish Civil War, among the thousand or more Cuban internationalists who took part in that fight. In our times, our compañero Commander Ernesto Che Guevara, the living example of the highest level of human being—as he himself so accurately defined a revolutionary—was born in Argentina, where he began his wanderings on the Rocinante that brought him to Cuba, then to Africa, and later back to the Americas, our common homeland, where he became immortal. It was precisely Che who, on instructions from our party, in 1965 established the first contacts with the MPLA and its leader, the renowned founder of the Angolan nation, compañero Agostinho Neto.

That's why those who in good faith ignore the historical precedents of our presence in Angola are mistaken when they search for its origins in naive geopolitical explanations drawn from the Cold War or East-West global conflicts—although there's no denying that even in the last century Martí viewed the independence of Cuba as a historical necessity to stop the neocolonial expansion which, he predicted, the United States would unleash against Latin America.

The Cuban presence in Angola was the continuation of the best traditions of our nation. If there was anything unusual about it, it was the people's massive participation, which had never before reached such levels; which unleashed the will of an entire people to take part in the epic struggle. Even more far-reaching and significant was the absolutely voluntary nature of their participation. Ours was not just a professional army, even if we take great pride in our troops' performance in combat and technical training. It was an army of the masses, a revolutionary army of the people.

The more than four hundred thousand Cuban men and women who passed through Angola over all these years and whose names will be honored by those who come after us, came from all the generations that are active today in the Cuban process—from Rebel Army veterans to the youngest recruits and reserve members.

All were motivated by a single interest—to come to the aid of and help consolidate our sister republic of Angola. As we pledged at the start, we didn't bring back with us anything other than the satisfaction of fulfilling our duty and the remains of our fallen comrades, with the exception of three whose bodies we have not recovered.

We must not forget another deep motivation. Cuba itself had already lived through the beautiful experience of the solidarity of other peoples, especially the people of the Soviet Union, who extended a friendly hand at crucial moments for the survival of the Cuban Revolution. The solidarity, support, and fraternal collaboration that the consistent practice of internationalism brought us at decisive moments created a sincere feeling, a consciousness of our debt to other peoples who might find themselves in similar circumstances. Compañero Fidel has emphasized those lessons from historical experiences in order to increase awareness of their importance. He awakened in the Cuban national consciousness the sense that as Latin-Africans we Cubans also had a historical debt to Africa, one of the vital roots of our nationality.

These were the authentic reasons for our people's response to the call for help from the young Angolan government, in accordance with international law. Angola's fate as an independent nation, its victorious anticolonial revolution were close

---

1. See glossary, Division General Samuel Rodiles Planas.

2. See glossary, Cuban independence wars.

"Cuba's presence in Angola was the continuation of the best traditions of our nation."

—Raúl Castro, May 1991

Cuba's revolutionary government extended internationalist support to independence struggles in Africa from the early 1960s on. In 1965 Ernesto Che Guevara visited Africa and met with leaders of national liberation struggles in Angola, Mozambique Guinea-Bissau, and Cape Verde.

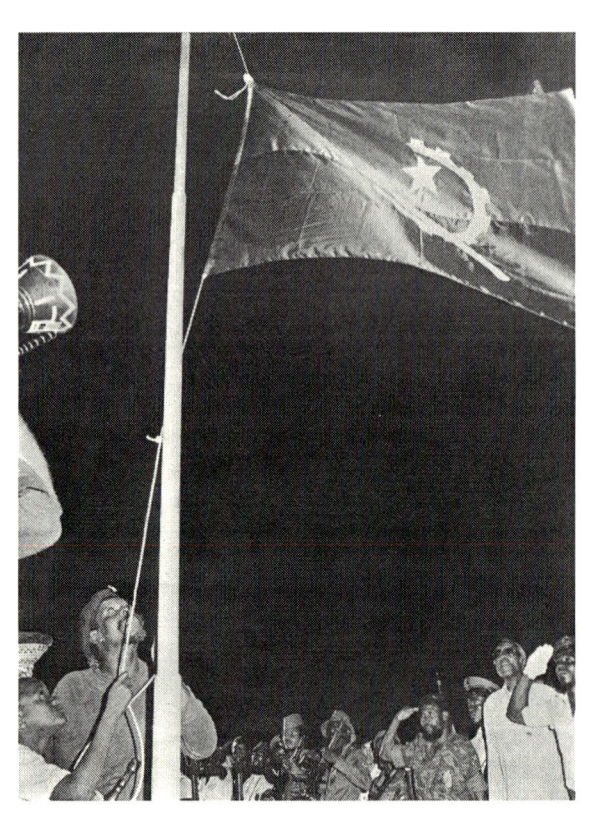

Top: Cuban medical volunteers with Guevara (second from left) in Algeria, July 1964. This was revolutionary Cuba's first internationalist mission in Africa. **Above:** Celebrating first day of Angola's independence, Luanda, November 11, 1975. **Bottom:** Guevara meets with Agostinho Neto (right) and other MPLA leaders during 1965 tour.

to being shattered by enemies attacking from the south, the north, and the east.

Imperialism, neocolonialism, and the mortal danger of the apartheid regime's expansion of its borders joined together to choke, at the moment of its independence, a potentially rich state whose creation was decisively influenced by people of progressive and revolutionary ideas.

Operation Carlota

In Cuba, we gave this internationalist mission the name "Carlota" in homage to an exceptional African woman who, on Cuban soil, headed two rebellions against colonial oppression and who—just as they wanted to do to Angola in 1975—was dismembered by the butchers who succeeded in capturing her during the second uprising [1843]. Without even knowing it, the thousands of Cubans who formed part of Operation Carlota were to spread the legend of the Cuban African heroine in Cabinda, Quifangondo, the Medunda hills, Cangamba, Sumbe, Ruacaná, Calueque, and Cuito Cuanavale.

Because of that unforgettable experience, our tank crews, infantrymen, artillerymen, combat engineers, sappers, pilots, special troops, scouts, communications troops, rear guard service personnel, antiaircraft defense troops, truck drivers, engineers, technicians, political workers, military counterintelligence, and combatants in other specialized roles in the Revolutionary Armed Forces and Ministry of the Interior—these compañeros will give the best of themselves. They'll become better patriots, better revolutionaries, and more committed party members. They—along with the outstanding and exemplary workers of Cubana Airlines and the merchant marine—were the ones who made the operation a success.

They served shoulder to shoulder with the Angolan people, together with teachers, doctors, construction workers and other civilian specialists from our country, through the longest, cruelest, and most devastating conflict that Africa has ever known. They were to be exceptional witnesses to the fact that no other people of black Africa has paid so dearly as Angola for the struggle to preserve its territorial integrity and its very existence as a state.

In the course of this extraordinary test, a decisive role was played by the commanders and officers who bore the brunt of countless decisions. They were called upon, above all, to set an example and indeed did so to the hilt, as evidenced by the fact that one out of every four of our men killed in action was an officer.

The serious threat that emerged in 1975 was not overcome until March 1976, following heavy fighting on the threshold of the Angolan capital. After the invaders were defeated they retraced their steps in the north, east and, above all, the south, when the South Africans crossed the border and entered their colony Namibia. We thought then that an opportunity for peace had opened.

On April 22, 1976, just a few days after the victory, we worked out with the Angolan government our first schedule for the gradual return of Cuban troops. And so, as Cuban civilian workers began arriving, the military contingent was reduced by over a third in less than a year.

But barely two years later, in 1978, the South African army again threatened Angola's security and territorial integrity and, of course, the lives of the Cuban internationalists working inside the People's Republic of Angola, south of the Cuban positions that defended a line two hundred fifty kilometers long on the border with Namibia. The dreadful massacre of Namibian civilians, mostly women and children, in Cassinga, where in May 1978 the South Africans murdered over six hun-

"We named this mission 'Carlota,'" said Raúl Castro, "in homage to an exceptional African woman" who led two rebellions against colonial oppression in Cuba. In 1843, in a slave rebellion at Triunvirato sugar mill in Matanzas province, she was killed and dismembered by the butchers who captured her.

dred refugees, was the most shameful episode.

In 1979, an apparent evolution of the situation led to Cuba and Angola again agreeing on schedules for the withdrawal of our troops. But these schedules were frustrated when South African aggression was again stepped up, combined with terrorist actions against Cuban civilian workers.

During those years, we had enough troops there to defend the established line and prevent any advance deep into Angolan territory. But in the strip that separated Angola and Namibia, the balance of forces favored the enemy. As long as this situation existed, Cuba and Angola never stopped searching for negotiated political solutions. We made this clear in the joint declarations

Cuban teacher Juana Martínez Rodríguez in Angola, 1988. "They served shoulder to shoulder with the Angolan people . . . through the longest conflict Africa has ever known," said Raúl Castro.

of February 1982 and March 1984. We rejected the efforts by the United States and South Africa to link Namibian independence to Cuba's withdrawal. We offered instead reasonable alternatives that were similar to those later included in the [1988] New York accords that brought peace to southwest Africa.

But before that, we had to defeat the South African army again.

Toward the end of 1987, thousands of South African soldiers were deployed against a FAPLA unit that was carrying out an important operation in southeast Angola. As the unequal battles developed, part of the Angolan unit came close to being surrounded and annihilated at Cuito Cuanavale. If the South Africans had been successful in their efforts there, the setback could have caused a collapse with consequences that could not be predicted.

At that moment the forces we had available in Angola weren't enough to address this situation—if we used them as reinforcements at Cuito Cuanavale, we could have ended up risking the overall stability of our defenses on the Southern Front. So reinforcements from Cuba became imperative. Moreover, it would have been wrong to insist on engaging in a decisive battle at Cuito Cuanavale because the terrain there had been chosen by the enemy; it was a place where the enemy had all the advantages. What was necessary was to organize an impregnable defense against which the enemy would wear itself down to no avail. Decisive actions should take place at a time and location chosen by us; that is, when we were the strongest and against their most vulnerable spots, concretely on the southwestern flank.

After rigorous consultations with the Angolan government and meticulous planning by the general staff of the Revolutionary Armed Forces, led by the commander in chief, on November 15, 1987, we made the historic decision to reinforce our troops in the People's Republic of Angola. This force, as you know, reached a total of fifty thousand soldiers. It was entrusted with the mission of fighting alongside Angolan troops to defeat the invading South African forces. Some day the time will come to explain how it was possible for a Third World country like ours to carry out this logistical and moral feat in a matter of weeks.

We know that the South African command estimated it would take us at least six months to transport the personnel, weapons, and combat supplies required for a division. By the time the South African strategists realized what we were doing, we had already doubled our overall forces and increased them many times over on the Southern Front. That gave us control of the skies there for the first time in twelve years.

To achieve this some real feats of labor were

"By the time the South African strategists realized what we were doing, we had already doubled our overall forces and increased them many times over on the southern front. That gave us control of the skies there for the first time."
—Raúl Castro, May 1991

JUVENAL BALÁN/JUVENTUD REBELDE

Top: Cuban tank battalion in Menongue, southern Angola, 1988.

Left: BM-21 multiple rocket launchers during operations alongside Angola's Brigade 25 in Cuito Cuanavale. These mobile units played a decisive role in pushing back the South African offensive, 1988.

PHOTOS: RICARDO LÓPEZ/GRANMA

Rapid mobilization of Cuban pilots, planes, and artillery to southern Angola in 1987 eliminated air superiority in south previously maintained by apartheid forces. **Left and above:** radar operators and ground crew supporting combat air operations, 1988.

necessary. This included building the Cahama airport in only seventy days, a step that put vital enemy targets within our reach.

We deployed a strike force on this front that included 998 tanks, more than 600 armored vehicles and 1,600 artillery cannon, mortars, and antiaircraft defense weapons.

From Cuba, in daily work shifts of up to twenty hours or more, just as he had done on several occasions since 1975, compañero Fidel personally directed the work of the general staff of the Ministry of the Revolutionary Armed Forces. He imbued in all of us the determination to achieve victory with a minimum of casualties, combining boldness and heroism with the philosophy of not risking the life of a single man without first exhausting all other alternatives.

"Our combatants in Angola—infantrymen, artillerymen, engineers, sappers, pilots, special troops, scouts, and all the others—will become better patriots, better revolutionaries, and more committed party members," said Raúl Castro. Above: Cuban sapper unit deactivates land mine at Cuito Cuanavale, 1988.

This spirit prevailed throughout these sixteen years. It became an ethic, a way of acting. It shaped the skill in fighting of the officers and it built a morale that increased both the confidence and the courage of the combatants.

Cuito held out. All the South African attempts to advance were pushed back. Their sophisticated long-range artillery kept bombing day and night. But it didn't frighten the Angolan-Cuban forces and turned out to be ineffective. Meanwhile, on the southwestern flank, a powerful group aided by SWAPO units was seriously threatening points of strategic importance to the enemy. The clashes with scouting detachments in Donguena and Tchipa, and the air attack on its positions in Calueque convinced the South Africans that it was impossible to win a military victory at the expense of Angolan sovereignty and against the combined Angolan and Cuban forces. Thus the possibility emerged for a negotiated settlement that would include the fulfillment of UN Security Council Resolution 435/78 for the decolonization and independence of Namibia, which had been put off so many times.

The December 1988 accords signed in New York, which are impossible to imagine without Operation Carlota, put the withdrawal of Cuba's internationalist troops in the context of an overall solution. And this from the start meant total withdrawal beforehand of the South African invaders, first from Angola and then from Namibia.

The timetable adopted as an appendix to the bilateral Cuban-Angolan accord for the organized withdrawal in stages of Cuban troops, with guarantees, has today been fulfilled ahead of schedule. Cuba's commitment not to stay there one day more than necessary has been honored. This is the latest gesture by the governments of Angola and Cuba toward contributing to a climate of trust, toward making a negotiated solution of the internal conflict irreversible.

Without the slightest intention of humiliating the adversary, nor to deny what each one of the parties contributed to the achievement of the accords, which we have fulfilled in a precise and exemplary manner, the peoples of Angola and Cuba are entitled to make the corresponding reflections on their victory.

It is a resounding victory to have stopped the initial onslaught and to have buried forever the myth of the invincibility of the South African army and the mercenaries. It is a victory to have helped our brothers and sisters to preserve Angola as an independent nation since 1975, for all these years. And it is a victory that today its security, its territorial integrity, and the inviolability of its borders are respected.

It is a historical victory to have won the independence of Namibia, the last colony in black Africa. Without this victory Namibia would have remained a colony and Security Council Resolution 435/78 would have gone unmet, buried in the UN archives despite SWAPO's heroic struggle.

It is a victory that affects the future. A new balance of power has been established in southern Africa. It is the product of the battles in Angola and Namibia, the progress made by the antiapartheid movement, and the political space won at the price of enormous sacrifices by the African National Congress and the black majority of South Africa in their struggle for a nonracist society and state.

It is a victory to have contributed to breaking the locks that held Nelson Mandela and other patriots imprisoned for more than a quarter of a century.

These victories also belong to all the peoples of Africa, to the governments that in defiance of substantial pressure collaborated to the extent of their possibilities to come to the aid of Angola. They belong to the Front Line states, the Organization of African Unity, the movement of Nonaligned countries, to all the peoples of the Third World.

It is impossible to understand the current political circumstances in Angola unless we take these victories into account.

The independent and sovereign government of the People's Republic of Angola has reached agreements in a negotiating process on the internal conflict. And it has done so despite South Africa's aggressive designs and invasions and despite crude meddling by Washington. This was possible only because the integrity of the Angolan state was maintained. It was possible only because the government in power is the legitimate government, heir to the anticolonial struggle that began February 4, 1961,[3] and it continues to lead the country and to offer the alternative of peace.

These accords should give rise to subsequent political processes. Whatever their results may be, if the accords reflect the will of the majority of the Angolan people, exercised with full and authentic liberty, it will also be thanks to these victories, because what the enemies of Angola always longed for was to wipe out the MPLA and the lucid, consistent, and brave leadership of President Neto and later compañero Jose Eduardo dos Santos.

Now that the mission that brought us to Angola has been accomplished, our only aspiration is that its people and their leaders can choose the paths along which the reconstruction and development of the country will take place without any kind of interference or pressure. Cuba will always, as it has throughout these more than fifteen years, respect the will of the Angolans.

It is not possible, however, to ignore the dangers that lie ahead as Angola exercises its national self-determination. Cuba is an exceptional witness to Washington's double-dealing in Angola, where it took upon itself the extraordinary role of both mediator and, at the same time, an active participant in the internal conflict. We know the countless demands the US made, always in favor of the interests of the aggressor.

The dominant role that the United States takes pains to play in the world today is not precisely the best guarantee for respect of the accords intended to bring stability and peace to the tormented people of Angola.

Compañeras and compañeros. In memory of our fallen comrades, we are gathered here to give an account to our people, to the leadership of the party and the government, of the mission assigned to the Revolutionary Armed Forces almost sixteen years ago.

When we face new and unexpected challenges we will always be able to recall the epic of Angola with gratitude, because without Angola we would not be as strong as we are today.

If our people know themselves better, if all of us know much better what we are capable of achieving—veterans as well as our young people, the new generations—that, too, is thanks to Angola!

The prestige, the authority, the respect enjoyed by Cuba today in the world are inseparable from

---

3. On February 4, 1961, the MPLA opened its armed action against Portuguese colonial rule, an attack by 250 combatants on the São Paulo fortress and police headquarters in Luanda.

"If our people know much better what we are capable of, it is because of Angola."

—Raúl Castro, May 1991

The rectification process in Cuba in late 1980s—which revived voluntary work brigades to build housing, schools, child care centers, and other facilities needed by working people—drew strength from volunteer internationalist mission of Cubans serving in Angola.

Above: Voluntary work minibrigade on construction project in Havana, February 1988. **Below:** Rally to inaugurate child care center built by voluntary work brigades, Havana, December 1987. Between 1986 and 1991, brigades built centers to provide care for 50,000 children.

what we accomplished in Angola.

Thanks to Angola, we understand in all its dimensions Comrade Fidel's point that when a people like the Cuban people has been capable of fighting and making sacrifices for the freedom of another people, what wouldn't it be capable of doing for itself!

If today we are more mature in our reflections and decisions, if today we are more staunch, more experienced, that too is thanks to Angola!

If today we are more aware of the work of the revolution, because we have experienced the disastrous remnants of neocolonialism and underdevelopment, for that we must thank Angola!

If today our political and ideological development, our revolutionary, socialist and internationalist consciousness are deeper, we owe that to Angola, too!

If today our combat experience has been enriched, if we're better trained and more ready to defend our nation, it is because together with hundreds of thousands of soldiers, 56,622 officers went through the school of life and struggle in Angola.

If our people are now prepared to confront any difficulty in the times ahead, if they're confident about themselves and their ability to resist, to continue developing the country, and to succeed, that confidence reflects our experience of how we grew in the face of adversity and won in Angola!

And if there's a people to whom we owe a lesson of stoicism, of greatness, of the spirit of sacrifice and of loyalty, it is the Angolan people, who said goodbye to our internationalist fighters in an exemplary manner, with love and gratitude.

Now, under our homeland's sky, the combat flag of the Cuban military mission in Angola is flying with honor next to our national banner with its single star. The glory and supreme merit belong to the Cuban people, the true protagonist of this epic, and history will judge its deepest and everlasting significance.

Allow me, on behalf of the Revolutionary Armed Forces, to say here, as Fidel did during the days of the October Crisis: Today more than ever I am proud of being a son of this people.

To our people and to you, commander in chief, I would like to report: Operation Carlota is now over!

PART II

An unparalleled contribution to African freedom

THE CRUSHING DEFEAT OF THE RACIST ARMY AT CUITO CUANAVALE WAS A VICTORY FOR THE WHOLE OF AFRICA

Nelson Mandela
JULY 1991

This speech was given in July 1991, barely two months after the last Cuban internationalist volunteers returned from Angola. Nelson Mandela had been released from prison a year earlier after more than twenty-seven years behind bars. He came to Cuba to thank the Cuban people for their longtime support to the struggle of the South African people. His remarks, excerpted here, were presented to tens of thousands of Cubans and international guests at the July 26 celebration in Matanzas, Cuba, marking the thirty-eighth anniversary of the attack on the Moncada garrison.

❦

First Secretary of the Communist Party, President of the Council of State and of the government of Cuba, President of the Socialist Republic of Cuba, Commander in Chief, Comrade Fidel Castro,

Cuban internationalists, who have done so much to free our continent,

Cuban people, comrades, and friends:

It is a great pleasure and honor to be present here today, especially on so important a day in the revolutionary history of the Cuban people. Today Cuba commemorates the thirty-eighth anniversary of the storming of the Moncada. Without Moncada, the *Granma* expedition, the struggle in the Sierra Maestra, and the extraordinary victory of January 1, 1959, would never have occurred.

Today this is revolutionary Cuba, internationalist Cuba, the country that has done so much for the peoples of Africa.

We have long wanted to visit your country and express the many feelings that we have about the Cuban Revolution, about the role of Cuba in Africa, southern Africa, and the world.

The Cuban people hold a special place in the hearts of the people of Africa. The Cuban internationalists have made a contribution to African independence, freedom, and justice, unparalleled for its principled and selfless character.

From its earliest days the Cuban Revolution has itself been a source of inspiration to all freedom-loving people.

We admire the sacrifices of the Cuban people in maintaining their independence and sovereignty in the face of a vicious imperialist-orchestrated campaign to destroy the impressive gains made in the Cuban revolution.

We too want to control our own destiny. We are determined that the people of South Africa will make their future and that they will continue to exercise their full democratic rights after liberation from apartheid. We do not want popular participation to cease at the moment when apartheid goes. We want to have the moment of liberation open the way to ever-deepening democracy.

We admire the achievements of the Cuban Revolution in the sphere of social welfare. We note the transformation from a country of imposed backwardness to universal literacy. We acknowledge your advances in the fields of health, education, and science.

There are many things we learn from your experience. In particular we are moved by your affirmation of the historical connection to the continent and people of Africa.

Your consistent commitment to the systematic eradication of racism is unparalleled.

But the most important lesson that you have for us is that no matter what the odds, no matter

---

This speech, and the remarks that follow by Cuban president Fidel Castro, are published in full in Nelson Mandela, Fidel Castro, *How Far We Slaves Have Come! South Africa and Cuba in Today's World* (Pathfinder, 1991).

"Cuban internationalists have made an unparalleled contribution to African independence."
—*Nelson Mandela, July 1991*

"Mandela paid the greatest tribute that has ever been paid to our internationalist fighters," said Fidel Castro at 1991 rally in Matanzas, Cuba, greeting the South African leader. ". . . At Cuito Cuanavale we helped resolve the problem of Angola's integrity and Namibia's independence, knowing that those fighting apartheid would also benefit from our struggles." Mandela's visit to Cuba came a year after his release from more than a quarter century in prison. By 1994 the white supremacist regime had fallen.

Above: Cuban president Fidel Castro and African National Congress president Nelson Mandela at July 26, 1991, rally in Matanzas, Cuba. **Below:** Workers demonstrate in Port Elizabeth, South Africa, August 1991. **Right:** Concert in Johannesburg, March 1990, greets Mandela shortly after his release from prison.

under what difficulties you have had to struggle, there can be no surrender! It is a case of freedom or death!

I know that your country is experiencing many difficulties now, but we have confidence that the resilient people of Cuba will overcome these as they have helped other countries overcome theirs.

We know that the revolutionary spirit of today was started long ago and that its spirit was kindled by many early fighters for Cuban freedom, and indeed for freedom of all suffering under imperialist domination.

We too are also inspired by the life and example of José Martí, who is not only a Cuban and Latin American hero but justly honored by all who struggle to be free.*

We also honor the great Che Guevara, whose revolutionary exploits, including on our own continent, were too powerful for any prison censors to hide from us. The life of Che is an inspiration to all human beings who cherish freedom. We will always honor his memory.

We come here with great humility. We come here with great emotion. We come here with a sense of a great debt that is owed to the people of Cuba. What other country can point to a record of greater selflessness than Cuba has displayed in its relations with Africa?

How many countries of the world benefit from Cuban health workers or educationists? How many of these are in Africa?

Where is the country that has sought Cuban help and has had it refused?

How many countries under threat from imperialism or struggling for national liberation have been able to count on Cuban support?

It was in prison when I first heard of the massive assistance that the Cuban internationalist forces provided to the people of Angola, on such a scale that one hesitated to believe, when the Angolans came under combined attack of South African, CIA-financed FNLA, mercenary, UNITA, and Zairean troops in 1975.

We in Africa are used to being victims of countries wanting to carve up our territory or subvert our sovereignty. It is unparalleled in African history to have another people rise to the defense of one of us.

We know also that this was a popular action in Cuba. We are aware that those who fought and died in Angola were only a small proportion of those who volunteered. For the Cuban people internationalism is not merely a word but something that we have seen practiced to the benefit of large sections of humankind.

We know that the Cuban forces were willing to withdraw shortly after repelling the 1975 invasion, but the continued aggression from Pretoria made this impossible.

Your presence and the reinforcement of your forces in the battle of Cuito Cuanavale was of truly historic significance.

The crushing defeat of the racist army at Cuito Cuanavale was a victory for the whole of Africa!

The overwhelming defeat of the racist army at Cuito Cuanavale provided the possibility for Angola to enjoy peace and consolidate its own sovereignty!

The defeat of the racist army allowed the struggling people of Namibia to finally win their independence!

The decisive defeat of the apartheid aggressors broke the myth of the invincibility of the white oppressors!

The defeat of the apartheid army was an inspiration to the struggling people inside South Africa!

Without the defeat of Cuito Cuanavale our organizations would not have been unbanned!

The defeat of the racist army at Cuito Cuanavale has made it possible for me to be here today!

Cuito Cuanavale was a milestone in the history of the struggle for southern African liberation!

Cuito Cuanavale has been a turning point in the struggle to free the continent and our country from the scourge of apartheid!

---

* Earlier at the July 26 rally, Mandela had been awarded the José Martí medal, the highest honor conferred on noncitizens by the Republic of Cuba.

THE MOST PROFOUND TRIBUTE EVER PAID TO OUR INTERNATIONALIST FIGHTERS

Fidel Castro
JULY 1991

It would not be right for us to emphasize Cuba's modest contribution to the cause of the South African people, but on hearing Mandela's speech, compañeros, I believe that he paid the greatest and most profound tribute that has ever been paid to our internationalist fighters. I believe that his words will remain, as if they were written in gold letters, as an homage to our combatants. He was generous, very generous; he recalled the epic feat our people performed in Africa, where all the spirit of this revolution was manifested, all its heroism and steadfastness.

Fifteen years we spent in Angola! Hundreds upon hundreds of thousands of Cubans went there and thousands more went to other countries. That was the epoch in which imperialism would have given anything to see Cuba withdraw from Angola and end its solidarity with the peoples of Africa. But our firmness was greater than all the pressures and was greater than any benefit our country might have gained had we given in to imperialist demands—as if there could ever be any benefit in abandoning principles and in betrayal.

We are proud of what we have done, and our troops came back from Angola victorious. But who has said this the way he has? Who has expressed it with such honesty, such eloquence? What we have not said, because basic modesty prevented us, he has expressed here with infinite generosity, recalling that our combatants made it possible for the sister republic of Angola to maintain its integrity and achieve peace; that our combatants contributed to the existence of an independent Namibia. He added that our combatants contributed to the struggle of the South African people and of the African National Congress (ANC). He said that the battle of Cuito Cuanavale changed the balance of forces and opened up new possibilities.

We were not unaware of the importance of the effort we made there from 1975 up to the last great feat, which was accepting the challenge of Cuito Cuanavale. This was at a distance greater than that between Havana and Moscow, which one can travel in a thirteen-hour nonstop flight. To get from Havana to Luanda is about a fourteen- or fifteen-hour flight, and Cuito Cuanavale was over in the southeastern corner of Angola, more than a thousand kilometers from Luanda. That was where our country had to accept the challenge.

As Mandela was telling you, in this action the revolution staked everything, it staked its own existence, it risked a huge battle against one of the strongest powers located within the Third World, against one of the richest powers, with significant industrial and technological development, armed to the teeth, at such a great distance from our small country and with our own resources, our own arms. We even ran the risk of weakening our defenses, and we did so. We used our ships and ours alone, and we used our equipment to change the relationship of forces, which made success possible in that battle. I'm not aware of any other time when a war broke out at such a distance between so small a country and such a great power as that possessed by the South African racists.

We put all our chips on the table in that action, and it was not the only time. I believe we did the same in 1975, when we took an enormous gamble sending our troops to fight the South African invasion of Angola.

I repeat: we were there for fifteen years. Perhaps it should not have taken so long, because the way

---

Excerpted from Castro's speech in Matanzas, Cuba, July 26, 1991, immediately following the remarks by Nelson Mandela.

we saw it, that problem had to be solved; simply put, South Africa had to be prevented from invading Angola. That was our strategic conception: if we wanted peace in Angola, if we wanted security in Angola, we had to prevent South Africa from invading Angola. And if we wanted to prevent the South Africans from invading, we had to assemble the forces and the weapons necessary to prevent them from doing so. We did not have all the equipment to do this, but that was our conception.

The truly critical situation occurred in Cuito Cuanavale, where there were no Cubans at the time because the closest Cuban unit was about two hundred kilometers to the west. This brought us to the decision to employ the troops and the weapons necessary—on our own initiative and at our own risk—and to send whatever was necessary, even if it meant taking it from here.

Cuito Cuanavale is the site that became historic, but the operations extended along a line hundreds of kilometers long, and out of these operations a movement of great strategic importance toward southwest Angola developed. All of this is symbolized by the name Cuito Cuanavale, which is where the crisis began; but about forty thousand Cuban and Angolan soldiers with more than five hundred tanks, hundreds of artillery pieces, and about one thousand antiaircraft weapons—the great majority of these antiaircraft weapons of ours were transferred from here—advanced toward Namibia, supported by our air force and an airstrip constructed in a matter of weeks.

I'm not going to speak here about the strategic and tactical details of the battles; I'll leave that to the historians. But we were determined, together with the Angolans, to put an end to the invasions of Angola once and for all. The events turned out the way we had foreseen—and we don't want to offend or humiliate anybody—because when this new balance of forces developed (and by then we had assembled troops that were invincible and unstoppable), the conditions for negotiations were created, in which we participated for months.

We could have waged big battles there, but given the new situation it was better to resolve the problem of Angola's integrity and Namibia's independence at the negotiating table. We knew—how could we not know!—that those events would have a profound effect on the life of South Africa itself, and this was one of the reasons, one of the motives, one of the great incentives that pushed us on. Because we knew that once the problem in Angola was resolved, the forces that were fighting against apartheid would also benefit from our struggles.

Have we said it this way before? No, never, and perhaps we never would have said this, because, in the first place, we believe that above and beyond whatever international solidarity the ANC has had, above and beyond the enormous support from abroad—of public opinion in some cases, of armed action in our case—the decisive and determining factor behind the ANC's successes was the heroism, the spirit of sacrifice and struggle of the South African people led by the ANC.

This man, in these times of cowardice and so many things, has come to tell us what he told us this afternoon. It is something that can never be forgotten and it reveals the human, moral, and revolutionary dimension of Nelson Mandela.

PART III

The Cuban Revolution was strengthened

THE PEOPLE OF CUBA WERE BEHIND OUR EFFORT

Armando Choy, Gustavo Chui, and Moisés Sío Wong
2005

Armando Choy, Gustavo Chui, and Moisés Sío Wong, three young rebels of Chinese-Cuban ancestry, became combatants in the 1956–58 revolutionary war that brought down the US-backed dictatorship of Fulgencio Batista and opened the road to the profound revolutionary transformation of Cuba. During the ensuing years of struggle each went on to become a brigadier general in Cuba's Revolutionary Armed Forces and served in multiple international missions.

WATERS: At various times between 1975 and 1991 all three of you served in Angola. Can you tell us a little more about this internationalist mission?

CHUI: The Cuban Revolution has been true to the legacy of the internationalists who helped us in the war for independence and in other struggles since then. Generals Máximo Gómez, who was Dominican; Carlos Roloff, who was Polish; Luis Marcano, who was Dominican; Juan Rius Rivera, who was Puerto Rican—all fought for Cuba's independence.

CHOY: Henry Reeve, "El Inglesito."

CHUI: Yes, the "Little Englishman," who was actually American.

CHOY: And Thomas Jordan, another American, who had fought in the US Civil War on the side of the Confederacy.

Throughout our history there were many internationalists who fought for our freedom. We have been true to their legacy.

When we carry out missions in countries that request our assistance, we have the opportunity to do what they did.

We lent assistance to the Congo, for example, and to the Republic of Guinea when Sékou Touré was president. At various times we also aided Guinea-Bissau, Cape Verde, Somalia, Ethiopia, Algeria, Syria, Yemen, Oman, Sierra Leone, São Tomé and Príncipe, Benin, Equatorial Guinea, and other nations in Africa and the Middle East.[1]

In terms of the Americas, there's Nicaragua, Grenada, and Guyana, among others, including Venezuela today.

We should stress that this aid has been of every type. It includes medical, construction, educational, and cultural assistance as well as military missions.

SÍO WONG: Our people hold socialist and internationalist ideas. That's how we've been educated. What other country can provide four or five thousand doctors for voluntary internationalist work when asked for help? But not only doctors. Our soldiers. The 375,000 Cuban combatants who served in Angola between 1975 and 1991 were all volunteers. That may not be well known, but it's a fact.

Each one was asked: "Are you willing to participate?"

"No, my mother's sick," someone might answer.

"Then you don't go," he'd be told.

It was genuinely voluntary. This was one of the conditions established by the party and Fidel. How can you risk your life for a just cause unless it's voluntary? There's no other way it can be done.

The battle of Cuito Cuanavale

WATERS: Nelson Mandela called the 1987–88 battle of Cuito Cuanavale "a turning point in the history of Africa." Yet outside Cuba—and much of

---

Reprinted from *Our History Is Still Being Written: The Story of Three Chinese-Cuban Generals in the Cuban Revolution* by Armando Choy, Gustavo Chui, Moisés Sío Wong (Pathfinder, 2005).

Africa—this battle is largely unknown.

Sío Wong: In late 1987 the enemy almost completely surrounded a group of Cuban and Angolan troops at Cuito Cuanavale. And the decisive battle took place there. The battle lasted more than four months, and in March 1988 the South African army was defeated. That defeat marked the beginning of the end. It forced them to sit down at the negotiating table. And they accepted an agreement.

Otherwise the offensive would have continued . . .

Chui: . . . which could have endangered their stability.

Sío Wong: Yes. And their defeat had a whole series of consequences—including the independence of Namibia and the release of Mandela after more than twenty-seven years in prison.

Chui: It "broke the back of the South African army," to use Fidel's words.

Sío Wong: How is it possible that the South Africans, with all their military and economic might, were forced to sit down at the negotiating table? From a strategic point of view, what we carried out was a deterrence operation. Our strategy was to concentrate a mass of tanks in southern Angola. How many tanks were there, Chui? Five hundred, a thousand? You'd have to look up the exact figures. It was a deterrent force, since it could have crossed into Namibia and continued southward.

The idea was always to do battle with the fewest possible casualties. How to accomplish that? Through superiority in the relationship of forces.

At one point in that operation our troop strength in Angola reached fifty thousand, equipped with artillery, tanks, and planes—80 percent of them deployed in the south. We built roads for our tanks and artillery. In two months we built an airstrip so our planes could provide cover for forces at the front, since the South Africans had a large number of aircraft. Up to that time, they had air superiority.

Leaders set the example

Waters: Compañero Chui, what were your responsibilities related to the Angola campaign?

Chui: Starting in September 1971 I was second in command of the 10th Directorate of the Revolutionary Armed Forces, the unit in charge of internationalist assistance. I served under Commander Raúl Díaz Argüelles, who had participated in Guinea-Bissau's war of liberation. In December 1975, barely a month after the start of our internationalist combat mission in Angola, Argüelles, who commanded our forces there, was killed by a mine, and I was named head of this directorate.

As Moisés mentioned earlier, I too had the honor of working under three leaders: Fidel, Raúl, and Almeida. I served under Almeida in the Sierra and am doing so again today in the Association of Combatants of the Cuban Revolution.

I served under Raúl in the Ministry of the Revolutionary Armed Forces from the time I was very young. He has educated and trained me. In the armed forces I was head of a number of bodies: Armaments, the 10th Directorate, and Cadres. I was also deputy chief of staff.

And beginning in September 1975, for two years I had the honor of working together with Fidel and Raúl in the Special Command Post to lead our forces during the first phase of the internationalist assistance to the people of Angola. The command post of what became Operation Carlota directed the dispatch and deployment of forces—first our instructors and then our combat volunteers—as well as supplies.

I acquired a lot of experience, not to mention Fidel's knocking some sense into me from time to time. But that's how you learn, and that's how leadership cadres are trained.

Koppel: When were you in Angola?

Chui: I was there briefly in 1976, and I later served from 1986 to 1988. As Mary-Alice said, Moisés, Choy, and I all served in Angola.

But not only that. The majority of the officers of the armed forces at that time took part in internationalist missions to one or more African countries.

---

1. The story of some of these early efforts is recounted in *Pasajes de la guerra revolucionaria: Congo* by Che Guevara (published in English as *The African Dream*, New York: Grove Press, 2000), *From the Escambray to the Congo* by Víctor Dreke (Pathfinder, 2002), and *Conflicting Missions: Havana, Washington, and Africa, 1959–1976* by Piero Gleijeses (Chapel Hill: University of North Carolina Press, 2002).

We gained experience in combat, troop organization, transport, and logistics. At times we did so together with the Soviets.

In 1977 I participated in establishing Cuba's military mission in Ethiopia, and I was also part of similar undertakings in Mozambique in 1977 and Nicaragua in 1979.

In 1986 I was named deputy chief of staff of the Cuban military mission in Angola, a responsibility I held until December 1987. At that time, on my request, I was named head of Operation 31st Anniversary—the reinforcement of Cuban troops and munitions for the battle of Cuito Cuanavale, which had begun in November. That operation was organized and directed by the commander in chief.

Sío Wong: I'll tell you a story that says something about Fidel's leadership of the Angola mission. In 1984 or 1985 Fidel went to the Soviet Union to attend the funeral of the Communist Party general secretary—I don't remember whether it was Andropov or Chernenko.[2] The room was filled with Soviet marshals and generals, who were wondering where Fidel had studied strategy, operational arts, military science. They had seen how Fidel directed the war in Angola and were astounded by it.

To organize an operation of this scope ten thousand kilometers away! And this wasn't a guerrilla operation. We were directing a regular war. How could a small country, without the great resources of the Soviet Union or the United States, supply an operation at that distance? How could it defeat an army such as South Africa's, along with the Zairean army and the mercenaries?

Chui is a witness. He was in the command center where, night after night, Fidel directed operations.

Fidel knew the terrain in Angola better even than those of us who were over there. "Go to such-and-such river, at such-and-such hill," he'd say in his cables. It was just like the Sierra Maestra, which he knew like the back of his hand. "Go to the top of such-and-such hill," he'd say. He would send a message to Che, to Ramiro [Valdés]: "Take such-and-such position." In Angola it was the same. He'd send a message to General Leopoldo Cintra Frías, who headed the military mission during the final stage: "Polo, position three tanks on such-and-such road. Don't let yourselves be outflanked."

Waters: Numerous ranking Cuban officers gave their lives in Angola. Chui mentioned Raúl Díaz Argüelles, his commander and head of the mission. Raúl [Castro], in one of his tributes to those who fell in combat in Angola, noted that a quarter of them were officers. Chui, you yourself were seriously wounded. How did that happen?

Chui: It was while my combat brigade was being transferred to Malanje province in northern Angola. On March 5, 1988, I was riding at the head of the third convoy, the one in which the weaponry was being transported. My vehicle set off a reinforced antitank mine, and I was thrown almost

COURTESY GUSTAVO CHUI

Gustavo Chui (front, center) reviewing Cuban tank brigade, Luanda, 1987. **Inset:** Chui's jeep, destroyed by antitank mine, March 5, 1988. Chui was critically wounded, losing a leg.

---

2. Soviet Communist Party general secretary Yuri Andropov died in February 1984. He was replaced by Konstantin Chernenko, who died in March 1985.

twenty meters. I was in critical condition.

Our commander in chief sent a plane to take me back to Cuba, given the gravity of my state. After quite a battle, medical science was able to save my life. But they had to amputate my right leg, which was in very bad shape. Typical of Fidel, he would ask about my health every day and gave precise instructions on what actions to take. I was treated first in the Brothers Ameijeiras Hospital by a very competent multidisciplinary team. Later, for my recuperation, I was transferred to the Center for Surgical Medicine Research, and I finished my rehabilitation at Carlos J. Finlay Military Hospital.

Sío Wong: In our army the leader is an example. We believe this is very important. This is also true for the revolutionary cadre. It's part of our code of ethics for cadres. The leader has to set an example.

This was always a characteristic of Che, who was incapable of giving an order he himself was not prepared to carry out. And it's equally true of Raúl and Fidel.

During the revolutionary war, as I mentioned earlier, compañeros had to write to Fidel asking him not to participate in combat. The same went for Raúl in the Second Eastern Front. Because Fidel and Raúl frequently put themselves at risk in combat. That's one of the reasons people follow them. It's a quality that Raúl has inculcated in our military leaders. They're first in combat, first in setting a personal example of austerity in the way they live.

The imperialists and counterrevolutionaries, including the Miami mafia types, have created a harsh and even bloodthirsty image of Raúl, but the truth is totally the opposite. I've known Raúl for more than forty years, seven of them working directly with him. He's a man of deep human sensibility. His entire life has been dedicated to fighting for the people. He's capable of attending to the country's most important problems while being attuned to the family and personal matters of individual compañeros and to what ordinary people face.

In private life, away from service, we're friends. I get together with his family, and sometimes my sister Angelita invites him over for a Chinese dinner. But at work he's the minister and I'm his subordinate. He's very straight and demanding.

That's why we've been able to organize armed forces with that discipline, devotion, dedication, prepared for anything. As Fidel has said publicly, Raúl is the organizer of a disciplined army, a proletarian army.

Choy: Raúl demands discipline—the same discipline he himself has. You see it in the way he dresses. Sometimes he demands that a person put his cap on, or button his shirt. But he himself follows the dress code of the armed forces strictly. His uniform is always buttoned correctly.

Cuba's strategic mission

Waters: During the time the Cuban volunteers were in Angola, you had to contend with UNITA, the Angolan force headed by Jonas Savimbi, which had South African and US backing. What was the approach of the Cuban armed forces toward UNITA?

Sío Wong: We didn't participate directly in Angola's struggle against the UNITA bandits led by Savimbi, who stood in the way of consolidating Angola's independence. We advised the Angolan armed forces, but we didn't participate in combat against UNITA.

We were there to help the Angolans, along with the Namibians, against South Africa's intervention, against aggression from the outside. Not to support any one of the groups within the country. It's important to state that clearly. We were very, very careful that our troops didn't directly participate in combat among Angolans.

Fidel has explained this numerous times. The strategic mission of our troops was to repel an invasion from South Africa and prevent an invasion from Zaire. We went no further than the border with Namibia. Internal problems must be resolved by those involved, by the belligerents themselves. That's always been our clear stand.

Choy: We fought UNITA only when UNITA attacked us. Our strategic mission was to prevent an invasion by South Africa or Zaire that would destroy the revolutionary, nationalist, independence process in Angola.

Chui: Civil wars are very cruel. Citizens of the same nationality, even family members fighting against each other.

Sío Wong: We also had to be very careful because, as Chui said, the Angolans had Soviet advisers as well as our own. It was very complex.

We had many arguments with Soviet military leaders concerning the structuring of the popular armed forces of Angola. Because their thinking and our thinking ran in two totally different directions. The Soviets were for creating large divisions, tank brigades, a classical army. But in our high command, Fidel insisted that the Angolans needed light units, not large units. That the jungle wouldn't accommodate big tank units.

In case of foreign invasion, we were there with small tactical groups. They were composed of an infantry unit, a tank unit, artillery, antiaircraft defense, designed to move very rapidly, with great maneuverability.

Moreover, we knew through our intelligence that the South Africans had seven tactical nuclear weapons. We had to take that into account. The Americans knew this too but permitted the South Africans to have them. A nuclear weapon wipes out a large unit at one blow. We had to have small units that would not be as vulnerable.

CHUI: We had to take into account the length of supply lines, too. Provisioning these smaller units wasn't as massive a job.

SÍO WONG: So we had long arguments with the Soviets, and we never came to an agreement. But time proved us right.

Negotiations with South Africa

KOPPEL: Compañero Choy, when were you in Angola?

CHOY: I served in Angola in 1980–81. I was deputy head of our Anti-Aircraft Defense and Air Force there. The commander in chief and the minister of the FAR also assigned me to work with my Angolan counterparts to organize Angola's antiaircraft defense and air force.

This wasn't an easy task, since it involved very close coordination with the Soviets. The Soviets sent the weapons and we sent the personnel.

KOPPEL: What did you do after returning from Angola?

CHOY: When I got back to Cuba in 1981, I held various leadership posts in the Anti-Aircraft Defense and Revolutionary Air Force.

In December 1986 the Council of State named me ambassador to Cape Verde, a position I held until 1992. During that time, on Sal Island, which is part of the Cape Verde Islands, the agreement with the South Africans was reached following their defeat in the battle of Cuito Cuanavale. The governmental accord was signed later at the United Nations in New York, but the basic agreement was achieved at Sal Island on July 27, 1988, between the South African, Angolan, and Cuban delegations. The essence of the agreement was that the South Africans would pull out of Angola for good, provided that Cuban armored units halted our advance before reaching the Namibian border and pulled back to a line north of the Cunene River, in southern Angola.

On the very day the Sal Island proposal was reached, the vanguard of General Enrique Acevedo's tank brigade, which was the forward detachment, had crossed the Cunene River. Behind it were a number of other brigades. We were practically at the Namibian border. The South Africans were in shock at this turn of events. There's an anecdote from the Sal Island negotiations.

As I mentioned, the South Africans had stated their willingness to leave Angola for good if Cuban military units stopped our march toward the Namibian border and returned to a line north of the Cunene River. The South Africans set the line. When the Cuban military delegation studied that line, they realized it was very close to the river. When it rained the area turned into a swamp, and the tanks wouldn't be able to move from there, posing the real danger that hundreds of these armored vehicles could become sitting ducks in case the war resumed. So our delegation offered to set a line even farther away from the Namibian border.

When this offer was made, the South African response was: "The Cubans aren't so bad after all!"

There was a second meeting at Sal Island a year or so later to review the implementation of the agreement. The South African delegation at that second meeting was headed by first vice minister of foreign relations Van Heerden, who dealt with the Angola question for them, plus four of their generals. Our delegation included General Leopoldo Cintra Frías (Polito) and myself.

The South Africans first tried to bribe us. Van Heerden began by explaining that South Africa was devoting 500 million rand [US$200 million] annually to "sustaining" Namibia. He said they were ready to continue giving Namibia this money provided there was peace at the border. What did that mean? That there would be no support for the African National Congress (ANC) and other movements in South Africa. They were practically asking us to commit a betrayal, in other words, and to pressure SWAPO [South West Africa People's Organisation of Namibia] to betray the antiapartheid struggle in South Africa. Of course, the political leadership of our country didn't agree.

At one point in the meeting, the head of our delegation, Carlos Aldana, turned to Gen. Cintra Frías and said, "General, please tell Mr. Van Heerden how much weaponry we've withdrawn."

Polito gave the number of men, artillery pieces, and tanks—eight hundred of them.

Van Heerden's mouth dropped.

He knew that even after that withdrawal, thousands of artillery pieces, tanks, other motorized vehicles, and men still remained with our forces in southern Angola.

"And what are you going to do in Cuba with so many tanks and so much artillery?" Van Heerden asked.

"They'll probably go to the Territorial Troop Militia" was our response.

His mouth was still open. Clearly the South Africans would have been unable to stand up to that force advancing toward the Namibian border.

All of Cuba behind Angola effort

WATERS: General Sío Wong, what were your duties?

SÍO WONG: I served in Angola in 1976. I was logistics chief for the military mission—a mission ten thousand kilometers away carried out by a small country.

I remember reading an article in the *New York Times* reporting that the US government was shocked at the operation we had carried out. It spoke about the extraordinary logistical support, saying Cuban soldiers in the trenches didn't lack even for Havana Club rum. That was a lie, of course. Maybe they were thinking about how US soldiers get their holiday turkey, their ice cream, and so on.

Support, yes. The combatants need a certain minimum of logistical support. We were able to do that because we are a socialist country. Within the bounds of our material limitations, all the resources necessary were made available.

You've got to give credit to the courage of compañeros who boarded the old Britannias. By the mid-1970s, when the Angolan mission began, those obsolete four-motor prop planes were practically out of service. We installed some additional fuel tanks so they could reach Sal Island off the coast of West Africa. They first had to make a stop in Guyana, then on Sal Island. So the trip to Angola by the first instructors was done in three legs. To fly in those Britannias you had to be brave, willing to risk your life. Later the Soviets approved the use of IL-62 planes for a number of flights, to transport some of our troops. There were ten flights during the early stages of the mission, I recall. I was on one of them.

We transported thousands of troops and large amounts of combat matériel. It was a secret operation utilizing a number of ports. We used our merchant fleet for sea transport. This could only have been done by a country like Cuba, with that type of spirit of solidarity.

I repeat: for these internationalist missions, we put the entire country behind the effort. Because we felt it was for something vital.

No, we didn't send bottles of Havana Club, but we did assure the essentials. We maintained a 10,000-kilometer supply line. That's something done by powerful countries such as the United States and Russia, countries with vast air and naval fleets. The US military, for instance, draws up contingency plans for its forces to wage wars on two fronts at the same time. They have the weaponry to do so. They have the supplies, the logistics.

As the one who headed logistics, I took a direct personal interest in the *New York Times* article I mentioned. But the effort was accomplished only because the entire country was mobilized behind it, with the goal of maintaining supplies for the troops. This chapter in our history has not yet been fully recorded, but it was a real feat.

From the human side, our troops went to Angola as part of an internationalist mission. That, too, was part of the anonymous work carried out by our people. They didn't ask where someone was being sent, nor could we tell them. A regiment would embark from the port of Nuevitas in Camagüey. So

PORT MARIEL'S 'PEANUT MEN'

Dockworkers at Port Mariel near Havana—two of the thousands of Cubans who kept the supply line running to Angola—recall with pride the contribution they made to the Angola mission at its opening in 1975. René Brito Gómez was brigade leader at Mariel.

RENÉ BRITO GÓMEZ

First we had to make a selection of the men—it couldn't be just anyone—a rigorous selection of those who could work. We would work twenty-four hours straight. Lots of ships! Lots of cargo! And we knew it was a question of time, gaining time. We knew the compañeros fighting round after round in Angola, helping in the liberation of Angola, depended in a big way on our efforts.

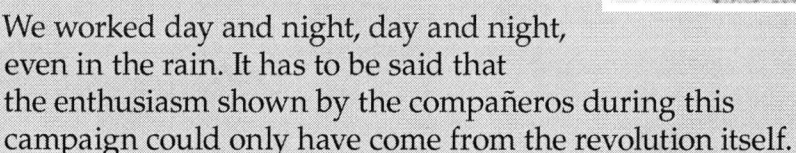

We worked day and night, day and night, even in the rain. It has to be said that the enthusiasm shown by the compañeros during this campaign could only have come from the revolution itself.

MAXIMILIANO L. VELÁZQUEZ

When we left our homes for the port, we said we were going to unload a boat hauling peanuts. That's why we called ourselves the "peanut men": there was no way we could tell our wives what we were really doing.

As we were ready to head out the door, the question would come:

"Where are you going?"

"We're going to unload a ship with a cargo of peanuts."

We spent months without returning home. Later, when we did come home, many dockworkers had problems because our wives thought we were out partying or dancing. Actually we were working; we knew we were fulfilling our duty. But only we knew this.

The dockworkers met this responsibility and we're ready, if necessary, to do it again.

From Milton Díaz Cánter, *Operación Carlota: Pasajes de una epopeya* [Operation Carlota: Reminiscences of a heroic feat] (Havana: Verde Olivo, 2006), pp. 33–34.

a story would circulate to the effect that the Havana regiment was going on maneuvers at the FAR's national live-fire range. The regiment would embark at night, in secret. It traveled without an escort. The vessel could easily have been sunk. Imagine a ship carrying a thousand soldiers that could easily have been attacked by a high-speed pirate vessel firing a bazooka blast. We were running a risk. That's why it had to be secret.

Someday the military academies will have to study this. How was it possible? Clearly it was the participation of the entire people.

CHUI: A base of support for this effort existed among the general population. That's without a doubt. The people could see the leadership vision that was being demonstrated. They had confidence in Fidel as a leader. Even though the battlefield was in Angola, they understood perfectly the instructions coming from here in Cuba. And they followed them.

"How was it possible for a small country to send supplies to a mission 10,000 kilometers away?" asked Moisés Sío Wong. "Clearly it was because we had the participation of the entire people." **Above:** Sío Wong, second from left, leading operation in northern Angola, 1976.

A turning point in history of Africa

KOPPEL: In the United States people know very little about what the Cuban Revolution has done to aid anti-imperialist struggles in Angola and elsewhere in Africa. But there will be a lot of interest in learning about this.

CHUI: We were a decisive factor during the 1970s in winning the independence of the Portuguese Empire's three major colonies on that continent—Angola, Mozambique, and Guinea-Bissau and the Cape Verde Islands. Nevertheless, these facts aren't stressed very much.

In the case of Guinea-Bissau, for example, the PAIGC [African Party for the Independence of Guinea and Cape Verde] led by Amilcar Cabral requested Cuban aid in fighting for the independence of their country. And our troops played an important part in the defeat of the Portuguese army, leading to the liberation of most of Guinea-Bissau by 1973. That event shook the Portuguese government, contributing to the "Revolution of the Carnations" in 1974. From this came a "domino effect" with the independence of the Portuguese colonies of Angola, Mozambique, and São Tomé and Príncipe.[3]

Choy knows this history well from the time he spent as ambassador in Cape Verde.

The case of Angola merits special attention. Our troops remained there fighting together with the Angolan people for more than fifteen years. Not only did we help defeat the South African army, but we also helped bring about the elimination of apartheid and the independence of Namibia.

From our efforts in Africa, the Cubans brought back nothing material for Cuba. Only our wounded and dead, and the satisfaction of a duty fulfilled.

SÍO WONG: History demonstrated we were right. We were not fighting just for Angola. From a strategic point of view, we were fighting against apartheid. And indeed at Cuito Cuanavale, after we broke the back of the apartheid army, they had to come to the negotiating table, grant independence to Namibia, free Nelson Mandela, and accelerate

---

3. The Portuguese dictatorship was toppled in April 1974 (see glossary, Portuguese revolution). Mozambique obtained its independence in June 1975. São Tomé and Príncipe became independent in July 1975; Angola in November 1975.

the process that soon led to the destruction of the apartheid system itself.

Angola strengthened Cuban Revolution

WATERS: What was the impact on Cuba itself? Not everyone agreed with expending such resources, with staying the course for so many years. How did the anti-imperialist struggle in Africa strengthen the Cuban Revolution?

CHOY: Well, it really strengthened us from an ideological standpoint. All of us who went had studied slavery, the exploitation of man by man, the exploitation of the countries in southern Africa. We had studied the evils that colonialism had wrought and was still creating. But we'd merely read about it in books.

In my own case—and I'm sure the same thing happened to other Cubans—I got there and could see with my own eyes what the colonial system really was. A complete differentiation between the whites, the Europeans—in this case the Portuguese—and the native population. We saw how these countries were exploited. We saw a country that was so rich, yet Angolans were living in what we saw as subhuman conditions. Because their country's riches were being stolen. Because the colonialists had not preserved the forests or the land.

Sometimes we'd be traveling in vehicles, and people walking along the road would run when they heard us coming. We learned why. Under Portuguese rule, if the native inhabitants didn't get out of the way, the colonialists would sometimes run them over. This went on for generations. So whenever they heard a vehicle coming, they'd run. And not just off to the shoulder of the road either. They ran because they'd been mistreated like this for years, for centuries.

The main lesson I learned from this mission was to fully appreciate colonialism's cruelty toward the native population, and the naked theft of their natural resources. To see a country with great natural wealth like Angola, yet with a population facing needs of the most basic type!

That's why I say that knowing the truth strengthened us from an ideological standpoint. The same thing happens whenever we see how a layer of the population in capitalist countries lacks the most basic necessities. The first time I went to Madrid, for instance, it was December. It's cold there that time of year. In the Gran Vía, the main street of that large city, I saw people sleeping on the sidewalk near a heating vent, with bags and newspapers over them.

You read about things like that in books, and you believe they're true. But until you see them for yourself, you can't fully understand the reality Karl Marx wrote about. That, I believe, is one of the lessons we all learned from internationalist missions.

These are the same lessons our doctors have learned, our athletic trainers, and other specialists who go to many countries. This includes countries that have natural riches, yet suffer tremendous backwardness and have great contrasts. The resources aren't used to help the masses of the people. And such backwardness isn't only in Africa. It's in the Americas too.

Bolivia, for example, has many tin mines. It has oil and natural gas. Nonetheless, it's tremendously backward. Ecuador the same, even though it's one of the principal exporters of oil. There are permanent social problems, because much of the population lives in virtually subhuman conditions. Until you see these realities, you don't understand how deep the problem goes. You don't understand what the people need. Direct contact with these problems strengthens our understanding. Those missions made this understanding concrete.

On diplomatic missions, you see this same reality from a different angle. I was able to see the kind of pressure Washington and other imperialist powers bring to bear on these countries.

Once I was talking about something to Cape Verde's secretary of state for cooperation, the equivalent of a deputy foreign minister. He was a good person with whom we had good relations. "The US ambassador spoke to me about this very problem," he told me, "and threatened that if our position was such and such, they would cut our economic aid." You read about things like this, but it's different when you hear them yourself. I had the chance to observe this when I was a diplomat. You can't speak out about these things publicly sometimes. I thought the Cape Verdeans should have made a statement, but they didn't. And these were friendly countries. But they avoided speaking publicly about something that would clash with US interests.

That's how it was.

CHUI: As Choy was saying, this experience helped all of us develop politically and ideologically. But the biggest impact was among the soldiers. In Angola and other countries of Africa, they could fully grasp the illiteracy, the misery, the lack of education, the lack of sanitary conditions and health care—conditions that people continue to live under.

COURTESY ARMANDO CHOY

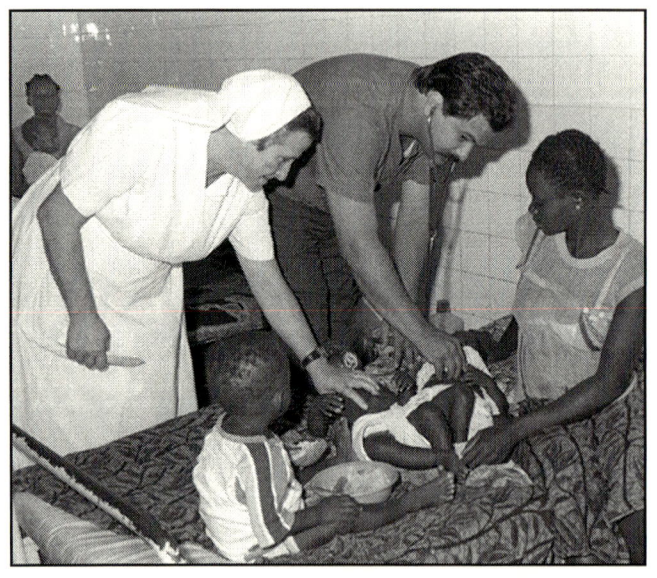

Top: Armando Choy (center, left) in Angola, March 1981. On far right is General Ramón Pardo Guerra. **Below:** Cuban doctor (center) at only hospital in Cabinda, 1987. Cuban medical brigade worked alongside personnel from Angola and other countries. "The main lesson I learned from this mission was to fully appreciate colonialism's cruelty toward the local population and the naked theft of their natural resources," said Choy.

Let me tell you a story. One time we slaughtered a pig, and I told one of the Cuban soldiers to give a piece of the leg to the Angolans. The Angolans said no, they didn't want it. When we asked why, they said they wanted the viscera, the innards. That's what the colonial masters always used to give them, and they had developed a taste for it. They really didn't like anything else. They weren't used to it.

Our internationalist combatants observed what people in these countries lack, things we don't lack in Cuba. They learned, in general, a whole series of lessons, and acquired valuable experiences about the inequalities and injustices of today's world.

There are many in the world who denigrate our stance of helping the peoples of other countries who are fighting imperialist oppression. But within Cuba it enabled us to consolidate the political and ideological development of the young people who went to fight and to assist other peoples, who understood the justice of their cause and were later proud of their mission. You couldn't find a better example of this than the Five Heroes being held prisoner by the empire because of the internationalist mission they were carrying out to defend the people of Cuba against terrorist attacks. They are part of this generation, and three of them served in Angola.[4]

SÍO WONG: On top of the things the compañeros have described, you have to add what our young doctors experience when they go to other countries. It sickens them. They see patients die before their eyes because the person doesn't have money. That's something that doesn't happen in Cuba. Such life experience means more than a hundred classes from a manual on Marxism. It's tremendous training for young people.

Right now we don't have any internationalist combat missions. We have other kinds of missions—as doctors, teachers, and more. But the simple fact that compañeros go and live in a capitalist country has a profound impact. This is something the three of us lived through growing up. But it's not something our young people today have experienced.

You can say many things to your children about

---

4. For the Angola experiences of Gerardo Hernández, Fernando González, and René González, see pp. 107–19.

what the past was like. When I was young, I recall, my brothers and sisters would tell me about the Machado dictatorship in the 1930s. They'd tell me about the big economic crisis of those years. But it's not the same as when you see, feel, live it yourself. If someone says, "Capitalism is like this; capitalism is like that," it's not the same thing. No, go live it. This is an experience for all our young people, because those who go—doctors, teachers, technicians, specialists—convey it to their entire family.

WATERS: Did the internationalist mission in Angola have an impact on Cuba's defense preparedness?

SÍO WONG: I wanted to talk about that aspect too, about how useful this was for us. More than 375,000 Cubans got actual combat experience in Angola. That's something the Pentagon has to take into account when they make their analyses.

Certain things are now being declassified, such as some of the previously top secret documents from the October Crisis of 1962. They reveal quite concretely how US leaders weigh their decisions. Kennedy asked the Pentagon chiefs how many casualties they would suffer in an invasion of Cuba, and they told him the estimate was 18,000 in the first ten days. The price would be very high. Very costly.[5]

During the October Crisis, as the commander in chief said, no one trembled or flinched. Our people are quite willing and ready, quite firm and determined.

That's what the Pentagon has to take into consideration.

---

5. This episode is described in *Making History: Interviews with Four Generals of Cuba's Revolutionary Armed Forces* (Pathfinder, 1999), pp. 30–32.

OUR VOLUNTEERS LEARNED WHAT CUBA USED TO BE LIKE

Luis Alfonso Zayas
2011

Luis Alfonso Zayas was one of the first group of recruits who in early 1957 reinforced the nucleus of the Rebel Army fighting the forces of the Batista dictatorship in the Sierra Maestra mountains of Eastern Cuba. He became a brigadier general in the Revolutionary Armed Forces of Cuba and a provincial government and party leader. He volunteered three times for missions in Angola.

WATERS: You volunteered for Cuba's internationalist mission in Angola on three occasions—at three different times, with different responsibilities. Start from the beginning. How did Cuba's aid to Angola begin and what were its aims?

ZAYAS: I first arrived in Angola in early December 1975. At that point, South African forces, backed by Washington, were just three hundred kilometers from the capital city of Luanda, coming from the south. They were advancing along a line extending from Porto Amboim to Quibala. They had a powerful force, with armored vehicles, artillery, planes, and infantry.

Approaching Luanda from the north, with another powerful force, was the FNLA, led by Holden Roberto, backed by the Zairean and US governments. They had been stopped just twenty kilometers away, in Quifangondo. They were practically at the gates of the capital.

And then there were the forces of UNITA, led by Jonas Savimbi. UNITA had the political and military support of the South Africans and Washington, which gave them weaponry and supplies of all types.

In response to this dire situation, Agostinho Neto, the president of Angola and leader of the MPLA, asked for Cuba's help. Cuba had supported the MPLA since 1965, when the guerrilla struggle against the Portuguese was in its early stages. If Neto had not requested Cuba's help, or if the Cuban forces hadn't arrived in time, the South African military would have captured Luanda. UNITA and Savimbi, or the FNLA and Holden Roberto, would have been installed as the government, thwarting the independence struggle of the Angolan people.

The people of Luanda supported the MPLA, which had led the struggle against Portuguese colonialism. But the MPLA did not have the organization or the means to stabilize the city's defense. It found itself in a corner.

With the support of the Cuban volunteers, the Angolan army—FAPLA, the Popular Armed Forces for the Liberation of Angola—turned them back.

KOPPEL: What were your responsibilities?

ZAYAS: I arrived in Angola in December 1975 to work with Jorge Risquet, assisting Agostinho Neto in the work of the party and government.

But that changed. As a result of the military situation, Angolan and Cuban troops were launching an offensive toward the north—toward a spot on the border with Zaire then called San Antonio do Zaire, today Soyo.

Close to midnight on December 31, we were meeting at the headquarters of the Cuban military mission to analyze this offensive operation. An officer was needed to coordinate actions between the Angolan forces—those of the FAPLA—and the Cuban forces that were there to give them support. I volunteered. Abelardo Colomé—Furry, as we know him—was the head of the Cuban military mission in Angola. Since I was working under

---

Reprinted from *Soldier of the Cuban Revolution: From the Cane Fields of Oriente to General of the Revolutionary Armed Forces* by Luis Alfonso Zayas (Pathfinder, 2011).

Risquet, Colomé told me I could go if Risquet authorized it, and he did.

That was around 1:00 a.m. By 4:30 a.m. I was on my way.

Risquet told me there were two compañeros who'd been with him earlier in Africa and would help me with anything.[1] I picked them up in a Cuban jeep and off we went, together with a driver and someone else in my escort. There were five of us. By later in the day we'd caught up with the Angolan force supported by Cuban tanks and artillery.

These troops had fought a battle against the FNLA and Zairean forces in Nambuangongo, some fifty kilometers north of Luanda. After the clash they had pulled back, and that's where we met up with them. Together we continued on, trying to get to Uíge province, then called Carmona. That's where Holden Roberto and the FNLA general staff were. We had to take a long roundabout route, since all the bridges along the coast had been blown up by the enemy. We maneuvered along some hills, by way of the road from Luanda to Carmona.

There were small groups of the FNLA in all the villages we passed through. But when they heard the artillery and tanks we were bringing, they fled. The FAPLA Ninth Brigade, which was with us, had a company of soldiers who'd formerly been commandos in the Portuguese army and fought very well. They were traveling in vans with the seats facing outward. When they arrived in those villages, they'd jump out from both sides and advance. Any remaining FNLA forces would flee.

One of the little villages along the highway was Quitexe. It was said that two FNLA companies were there, along with a company of white mercenaries from Portugal and other countries.[2] In that village heavier combat took place. The battle lasted several hours, with the FNLA forces suffering a number of casualties.

After we took Quitexe, we continued on to Carmona [Uíge], a town about two hundred kilometers from the coast. When we got there, it had already been taken by another FAPLA column coming from the other direction and led by Commander Víctor Schueg Colás, a Cuban. After a fight, the FNLA had retreated toward the north.

We then headed west in the direction of Ambrizete—today it's called N'zeto—and Ambriz, two small villages along the coast. Between Carmona and Ambrizete, the Portuguese had built an immense dirt landing strip, which French and Belgian NATO troops had been allowed to use as well. The FNLA had forces in a little village there, supported by a company of white mercenaries. We fought them and took the village and airstrip, including warehouses full of weapons and ammunition, as well as nine very large napalm bombs. A mechanized battalion that Fidel had sent to support Schueg's column joined us there and continued on with us to Ambrizete.

The enemy forces in Ambrizete were supported by a company of white mercenaries, plus some Koreans who were experts in blowing up bridges. As the enemy retreated over a very long and high bridge spanning the fast-flowing Mbridge River, they blew it up. We were unable to cross and had to wait for a raft to be brought up from the south. We couldn't move all the military equipment for about two weeks, when they brought a *changada*, which is a barge with two engines.

By that time Schueg had arrived at San Salvador province—today it's M'banza Congo. This is Angola's northernmost province, except for Cabinda. It's on the border with Zaire. The FNLA leadership was still in that region, along with about forty or fifty white mercenaries. A number of mercenaries were killed, and Callan, their main leader, was captured. Later he was tried and executed.[3] We continued ahead from the south, along the coast, to San Antonio do Zaire. There one mercenary died in

---

1. From August 1965 to January 1967, Risquet headed a contingent of Cuban internationalist combatants in the former French colony of Congo-Brazzaville. Known as Column 2, this detachment was originally conceived as a support unit for Column 1, led by Ernesto Che Guevara, which was working to assist liberation forces in the former Belgian colony of the Congo. Risquet and the leadership of Column 2 were given responsibility for initiating collaboration with and aid to the MPLA.

2. Describing the conduct of these mercenaries and the FNLA forces toward the Angolan population, the January 30, 1976, *New York Times* said: "Refugees report that these towns . . . have been completely sacked and that their populations have fled. . . . The Zaire army units were said to have been the most active in the looting."

3. "Colonel Callan"—not, in fact, a colonel—was a Cypriot named Costas Georgiou who had been a British paratrooper dishonorably discharged and jailed for robbing a post office in Northern Ireland.

combat and their second in command, John Baker, was captured.

We left Luanda on December 31, 1975, and reached the banks of the Congo River, dividing Zaire from Angola, more than a month later, on February 7, 1976. We celebrated the liberation of the north with a flag-raising ceremony attended by four members of the MPLA Political Bureau, including Lúcio Lara and Iko Carreira. My ten days had turned into almost six weeks.

After that I stayed on to train the Angolans, so we could turn over to them the tanks, artillery, and BM-21 rocket launchers we'd brought. In April 1976 all the equipment was handed over to the Angolans.

I then returned to Luanda to help organize a parade to commemorate the anniversary of the establishment of the Angolan armed forces on August 2, 1974. There had never before been a parade on that scale in Luanda.

At the end of 1976 I returned to Cuba.

WATERS: After the success of the operation in the north in early 1976, did this part of Angola remain under government control, or were there other battles in this region later?

ZAYAS: At that time, in 1976, the north was considered liberated. It was in the hands of the MPLA. That's why Holden Roberto left Angola and went to Zaire. He was in the pay of the CIA and lived in Zaire, where he was married to a sister-in-law of dictator Mobutu Sese Seko. Later there were other complications, and the fighting continued.

KOPPEL: What about the charge that Cuba was intervening in an internal struggle among Angolans?

ZAYAS: It's true there was a conflict between different organizations in Angola: the FNLA, the MPLA, UNITA, the FLEC—the Cabinda Enclave Liberation Front. But the Cubans didn't interfere in it.

In part the divisions were regional, based on tribe. In the northern region, people generally supported the FNLA. In the southern areas, people supported UNITA. And in the central region they supported the MPLA. In Cabinda, people were with FLEC.

But what was really involved? UNITA and the FNLA were backed by Zaire, the South Africans, and the US government. So it was no longer just a struggle among Angolans. What was involved was imperialist intervention to thwart Angolan independence and take control of Angola as the Portuguese withdrew.

As for the Cubans, we were defending Angola from aggression by South Africa above all, but also by Zaire—both backed by Washington. We didn't get involved in the internal struggle among these organizations. That was a problem among Angolans. It was something for them to resolve.

WATERS: When did you return to Angola?

ZAYAS: As I said, I came back to Cuba in late 1976. But in early 1977, after I'd been in Cuba about two months, Risquet asked me to return to Angola.

At Angola's request, Cuba was stepping up collaboration on all levels at that time. Cubans were helping in education, in construction, in public health—in every area. By 1977 there were about three thousand Cuban civilians working in Angola, in sixteen of Angola's eighteen provinces.

So we created a central leadership structure of the Cuban personnel in Angola, both on a national level and in the provinces. That's what Risquet asked me to help with. I was basically second in command to Risquet for everything involving the civilian missions—supplies, relations with the Angolan government, and so on.

For this I had to visit all the provinces. I went as far south as Cuando Cubango—which is two and a half hours by plane—to take supplies and to establish the mission there. Ten or twelve compañeros were going to work in that province, which was UNITA's stronghold. That's the region where the battles in Cangamba and Cuito Cuanavale took place later in the war.[4] UNITA came to have a powerful army there, backed by the South Africans and with the support of US imperialism.

On May 27, 1977, a few months after I arrived for my second tour, there was an attempted coup against the leadership of President Neto. Nito Alves was the leader of that counterrevolutionary uprising.

Alves was Angola's minister of the interior. His influence extended throughout practically the entire country, since he appointed the provincial commissioners, who were in fact the government

---

4. Cangamba was the scene of a seven-day battle in August 1983 in which some eight hundred FAPLA and Cuban combatants, without food or water, battled more than three thousand UNITA troops and dealt them a decisive defeat.

"At Angola's request, Cuban volunteers were helping in education, construction, public health, in every area. By 1977 there were 3,000 Cuban civilians working in Angola."

—*Alfonso Zayas*

"Wherever a doctor shows up," Fidel Castro told the first contingent of volunteers leaving for Angola in September 1975, "his services will be needed right away." Under Portuguese rule, Angola had only 90 doctors. After independence, all but 30 left.

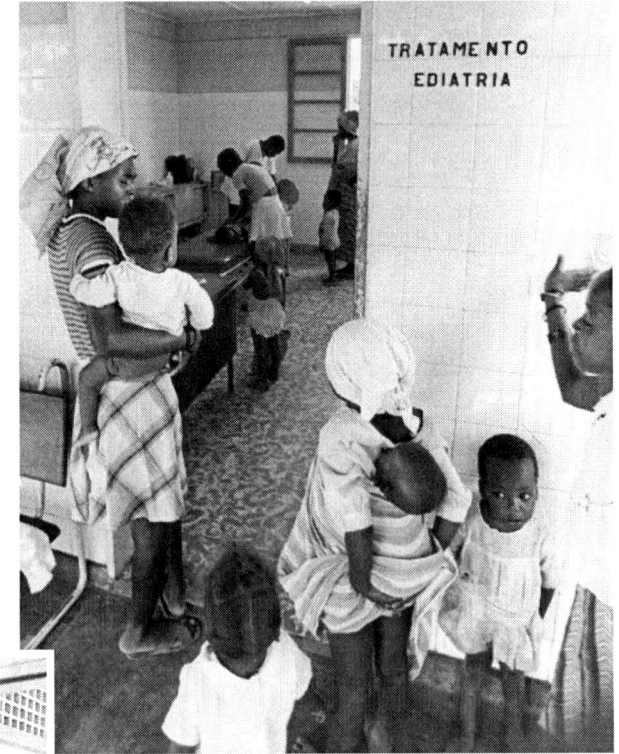

PHOTOS: BOHEMIA

Above: Pediatrics ward in Luanda hospital, staffed by Cuban personnel, 1976. **Left:** Anatomy class at Luanda Hospital nursing school in 1976, with Cuban teacher.

PHOTOS: GRANMA

Over the course of the 1975–91 mission, more than 50,000 Cuban civilian volunteers served in Angola. **Left and above:** Cuban teachers in Angola in 1983 and 1988, respectively.

in the provinces. Alves had the support of the people he'd appointed. At one point, it was not the MPLA that was governing but Alves's faction within the MPLA—the "microfaction," as it became known.

Several members of the MPLA Political Bureau were involved. These included Monstruo Inmortal [Immortal Monster]. His real name was Jacobo Caetano. He was a member of the Political Bureau, FAPLA's chief of operations, and practically Neto's right-hand man. There was also Bakaloff—Eduardo Evaristo—who was FAPLA's political head.

In other words, the counterrevolutionary coup leaders included the army's political head, its chief of operations, the minister of the interior, several other ministers, and nearly all the commissioners in every province.

What happened?

Alves's forces took over the government radio station in Luanda. That station played a decisive role, since it was one of the few sources of information and people followed it closely. Its broadcasts from Luanda were rebroadcast and networked to all the provincial radio stations. The microfaction began attacking the MPLA over the air. That was the beginning of the action.

They put a Pioneer on the air to speak.[5] Actually, he wasn't a Pioneer, but he was young and that's how they presented him. They'd given him a piece of propaganda criticizing Neto to read aloud, which he did. Until then they'd criticized the MPLA but said nothing about Neto.

The radio station called on people to go to the presidential palace, the seat of government. And people headed there.

KOPPEL: What was the response of Cubans there collaborating with the Angolan government?

ZAYAS: The Cubans didn't know who was who, or what was what. But there were Cubans in each of the provinces, and the heads of our civilian missions knew the problems there. They had good relations with the provincial commissioners, with the FAPLA, with the Ministry of the Interior, with the security forces.

When the Cubans working in each province heard what was happening, they immediately said,

"No way!" One of these was Rafael Moracén, the Cuban adviser to the commander of Neto's presidential regiment. When coup supporters heeded the call over the radio to go to the presidential palace, they were met by this regiment, which turned them back.

Moracén, with Angolan and Cuban forces in tanks, then headed to the radio station. Having taken the station, the microfaction practically had power in its hands, since they could issue directions heard everywhere. But Moracén's brigade retook the station.

I was at the Hotel Presidente at the time, recording the radio broadcasts. "What's going on here?" you could hear Moracén saying when he arrived at the station. "You there, what are you saying about Neto? Neto is the president here!" You could hear his voice: "Neto is the president here!" That's what Moracén said.

After the radio station was retaken, things calmed down.

A decisive role was played by those heading the Cuban civilian mission in each province, along with the Cuban armed forces there. They kept the situation under control. We had great influence at every level, beginning with Neto, who was very appreciative of the aid provided by the Cubans. And we had influence in the provinces, too. Because of the role we'd played in defeating the South African invasion, Cuban collaboration was accepted. When asked for advice, we gave it. We voiced our opinions—very tactfully—and the Angolans we worked with were quite receptive.

WATERS: What were the differences between the Neto leadership and the microfaction? What was behind the coup attempt?

ZAYAS: Lust for power and riches. Angola has oil, it has gold, diamonds, everything. It's a country with immense mineral wealth.

WATERS: Fidel has talked about the differences between Cuban and Soviet advisers in Angola. What was your experience?

ZAYAS: The Soviets had some advisers in Angola, although not many. They had a different strategic military conception from ours. The Soviets favored big armies. What was needed in Angola, however, wasn't big armies or grand military strategies. The help they needed was much more practical.

The Soviets did give a lot of support in weap-

---

5. The Pioneers was a children's organization set up by the MPLA in 1975.

"Fidel led the war as if it were here in Cuba," recalled Alfonso Zayas. "He knew what was happening in every corner of the country. He received information every day from those of us who were over there." **Above:** Fidel Castro explaining military situation in Angola, 1976.

onry and equipment. It was for Angola, but it was handled by the Cubans. Why? Because few Angolans knew how to use most of it. They had to be trained. Plus the Soviets had experienced setbacks in Africa before, where they'd sent arms and support that had been lost to the enemy or abandoned. That's why the Soviet weaponry was handled by the Cuban force.

Many Angolan technicians and armed forces personnel were trained here in Cuba. The Soviets also provided training to the Angolans—to pilots, combat engineers, communications personnel, and so on—teaching them to use the equipment. They trained a lot of Angolan military personnel in Russia. But the Angolans generally accepted the Cuban advisers more readily than the Soviet ones. They understood our advice better, since it was more practical, more in tune with the needs and character of the struggle in Africa.

WATERS: What about Fidel's role in leading the Angola operation?

ZAYAS: Using a map of Angola, Fidel led the war as if it were here in Cuba. He knew what was happening in every little corner of the country. He received information every day from those of us who were over there and from his liaisons, who would come and go.

Sometimes Fidel knew things you wouldn't even imagine, and he'd give instructions for what had to be done. "Do this, do that, because the South Africans are going to do such-and-such." And he'd be right. Fidel directed the battle of Cuito Cuanavale against the South Africans, as if he were in the forward command post in Angola.

The big decisions to send forces to Angola were made by Fidel. The US government never imagined Cuba could send fifty thousand armed men to fight in Africa. How could Cuba do so, since we had no transatlantic merchant ships set up for troop transport, nor did Angola? But we Cubans, of course, are prepared for the greatest sacrifices, and that's how our forces were able to be sent to Angola. All of Washington's great strategists couldn't even conceive of that.

How was it possible to send thousands of men aboard aged turboprop passenger planes and merchant ships? On board the freighters, they had to travel in the cargo hold. The men couldn't go on deck or they'd be spotted. But then how do they relieve themselves? How do they bathe and wash up? How do they eat, since the ship wasn't set up to provide meals for thousands of men? To spend three weeks like that, who can bear it? You need to have the kind of consciousness the Cubans who went had.

Their spirits were high, because they had confidence in Fidel. Fidel tried to meet with every group of soldiers that left. He'd go and talk to them. He'd explain what the situation was. And if he couldn't go himself, he'd send someone else.

Only with a leadership like Fidel's could something like that be achieved.

Our forces arrived in Angola in November 1975, right when they were needed. It was the same in 1987, with those needed during the siege of Cuito Cuanavale. Because in both cases, there was no force in Angola capable of taking on the advancing South African troops. Fidel made the decision to send what was needed to win, and they arrived in time to achieve that.

Fidel led everything that had to be done to defeat the South African forces. He'd spend entire nights analyzing and figuring out what had to be done and how. His direct participation was decisive.

KOPPEL: What about the civilian mission you were helping to lead?

ZAYAS: By the time I left Angola in 1978, there were, as I said, more than three thousand Cuban civilian collaborators. Most were in health and education, although there were some in every sector.

WATERS: How long would they volunteer for?

ZAYAS: They'd generally go for two years. Some went for one year, but most often two. I'm talking about the civilians. Soldiers also went for two years, but they stayed longer if they had to. The soldiers were volunteers too, but they acted under orders. The civilians committed to two years and after that went home. There was a rotation to send replacements.

The civilian volunteers got one month of vacation each year, in Cuba. That involved transportation and planning. It wasn't easy, given the involvement of all the various bodies in Cuba sending people there. When volunteers completed their mission, replacements were sent to continue the work they were doing. The Cuban agency Cuba Técnica played an important part in organizing all this.

Nor were all the Cuban volunteers in Luanda, of course. It's in Luanda that we prepared the conditions to receive the arriving Cubans and send them out to the provinces where they'd be serving. Transport was generally not by land, since UNITA had laid a lot of land mines. Road travel could only be done in caravan, with military support. Most travel was by air, and all that had to be planned and coordinated, including with the Soviets, who had cargo planes there. Cubans had to be transported in those planes, sometimes sitting on top of cargo all the way to the provinces.

Washington never imagined Cuba could send thousands of men to fight in Africa, said Alfonso Zayas. "Our forces arrived right when they were needed." **Above:** Armored vehicle returning to Cuba after defeat of South African forces, 1988.

By 1978, as everything was getting better organized, the technical assistance agency I mentioned was created—Cuba Técnica. At the time, it was under the Ministry of Foreign Relations. Now it works under the direction of the Ministry of Foreign Investment and Economic Collaboration.

Eventually, Cuba's collaboration was formalized in agreements, but initially it was all done on the fly. Angola would ask, and we would send.

WATERS: From 1985 to 1987 you were in Angola a third time, now heading the Cuban civilian mission in Cabinda, a province in the north separated geographically from the rest of Angola. What was special about that experience?

ZAYAS: Cabinda's status is the result of centuries of colonial plunder and imperialist domination. At the 1885 Congress of Berlin, the European colonial powers divided up Africa among themselves. So the Belgian monarchy could have sea access for its landlocked colony in the Congo, the imperialists signed treaties that cut a sliver through Portugal's colonial possessions. That's how the northern province of Cabinda came to be geographically separated from the rest of Angola. In exchange, Portugal was given a piece of territory in the east—an area rich in diamonds, close to the border with present-day Zambia—for its colony of Angola.

Cabinda is the center of Angola's oil production. Since liberation in the mid-1970s, the entire country has lived off export earnings from that oil. The main company operating there was Gulf Oil.

KOPPEL: In countries like Equatorial Guinea, due to the legacy of imperialist domination, very few people have the technical knowledge and education demanded by the oil companies. Management brings in trained personnel from the United States, from Europe, and from other imperialist countries, employing relatively few Equatorial Guineans. Was that also true in Cabinda?

ZAYAS: There were people from many countries working there, but very few from Cabinda itself. The majority came from other countries, from all over. There were even Cubans

"Washington's great strategists couldn't even conceive of the kind of consciousness the Cubans demonstrated in Angola," Alfonso Zayas said. **Above:** Zayas (left, with sunglasses) on plane with Angolan military leaders, including João Luís Neto (right, reading newspaper), vice minister of armed forces, known by his nom de guerre, Cheto, 1976. Zayas served three tours of duty in Angola.

who lived outside Cuba working for Gulf Oil.

WATERS: Are the people of Cabinda from a different tribe than in other parts of northern Angola?

ZAYAS: Yes. A large part of Cabinda's people are from some of the same tribes as people in Congo-Brazzaville and the Democratic Republic of Congo, from whom they are separated by borders long ago drawn by the imperialist powers. They don't necessarily understand each other, however. They speak different dialects.

FLEC, the Cabinda Enclave Liberation Front, was active in that province. It was a tribe-based separatist movement supported by Zaire, and later by UNITA. The US government also supported it.

When I got to Cabinda in 1985, there was fighting between FLEC and the MPLA/FAPLA. FLEC was carrying out attacks on the provincial government in Cabinda, on the airport, for example. UNITA forces there were said to be giving support to FLEC. Sometimes you couldn't leave the provincial capital without protection of the armed forces. There was always danger of attacks.

KOPPEL: What were your responsibilities in Cabinda?

ZAYAS: I was head of the civilian mission overseeing all the internationalist collaborators in Cabinda from the different bodies, in health, education, communications, and so on.

Cuba's civilian collaborators in Angola were organized in contingents, by province. One of my responsibilities, for example, was to work with the forestry contingent in Cabinda. There were about four hundred forestry workers cutting timber in the Mayombe jungle there. The lumber was for export wherever the Angolans wanted to sell it, but most was bought by Cuba.

There was no way to transport the lumber by sea, however, since Cabinda doesn't have a port and is separated from the rest of Angola. The nearest port was Pointe-Noire in Congo-Brazzaville.

A tax had to be paid to the Congo government, and there was never money to pay it. So most of the lumber wasn't exported. A lot of very good timber was lost.

WATERS: How many Cubans were in Cabinda at that time?

ZAYAS: There were about six hundred Cubans on civilian missions, including the forestry contingent, doctors, teachers, and others.

We had Cuban advisers working in every government body. Cuba's Ministry of Public Health had people there to provide medical care. It was very difficult, since there wasn't enough medicine, but the Cuban doctors did wonders. There were Russian doctors too. Different specialties were covered by either Russians or Cubans. If there was a Russian orthopedist, for instance, there wouldn't be a Cuban one, unless there was a need for both.

The medicine that was needed didn't always come, so we had to ration it. Supplies for the population were sent mostly by plane, from Luanda. Some things were sent by *patana* [small boat]. Since there was no port, they came ashore on the beaches.

One thing I was asked to do—using my experience in party and government work in Las Tunas and elsewhere—was to come up with a master plan for Cabinda. A plan for agricultural production, industry, urban development, everything. That's what I was working on, and I sent for experienced planning personnel from Cuba. We ran into lots of problems due to Cabinda's level of development.

First, they didn't have the resources. I'm talking about resources of all types, human as well as material. They lacked a trained workforce. You can't put up a building using unskilled construction workers. There has to be an architect. You have to have skilled bricklayers.

I'm giving the example of constructing a building, but it's the same with any project. To build a road, it's necessary to have a plan, the right personnel, and the funding to carry it out. Without state support and planning, it can't be done. Since Cabinda has no port, to give another example, everything had to be brought in by plane, or through Pointe-Noire in Congo-Brazzaville. In all these cases, the resources were lacking.

Another problem was the view in Cabinda that it's better to import than produce. Some would even argue it's better to import chickens than to raise them, for instance. And in a certain sense, they were right. The Portuguese had chicken farms there, with incubators and all the supplies needed to raise chickens.

But when any of these things were in short supply, the poultry would die; everything would be lost. So they'd say it's better to import chickens, eggs, all of it.

WATERS: Import from where?

ZAYAS: They imported chicken, eggs, and meat from the Netherlands and elsewhere, for example. They bought products from France and other countries. They'd bring things in from Pointe-Noire in Congo-Brazzaville.

In fact, people in Cabinda largely survived through barter across the borders with Congo-Brazzaville and the Congo. They exchanged malanga—which is a tuber they grew—for clothing, for manufactured articles, and for other food. People mainly fed themselves off what they grew. They cultivated small parcels of land, minifundia. While there are vast tracts of land in Cabinda, there are no big farms or ranches. Cattle graze in the wild. There's little agricultural development.

Those who cultivate the very small plots are mostly women. It's considered women's work. Often you'd see a woman carrying two loads on her back, a bundle of firewood for cooking, plus a child.

KOPPEL: How do you size up your mission in Cabinda?

ZAYAS: Even with all the limitations, what we accomplished was positive. My mission was to try to help develop Cabinda in terms of productivity, as well as to make sure that what the Cubans did there was done right, starting with the humblest Cuban collaborator wherever he was—like doctors at the side of their patients, for example.

Many things had to be done, so Cubans there understood the role each of them had to play. And we achieved that during the two years I was in Cabinda, in addition to helping in every way possible the party and government there.

We didn't accomplish everything we wanted to do, but we fulfilled our mission. And we were grateful, since every day one learns more. Every day one gets a better understanding of the world.

WATERS: Among the hundreds of thousands

"We go to help, to teach, to collaborate," says Alfonso Zayas about Cuba's internationalist missions. **Above:** Cuban volunteers await deployment after president Fidel Castro offered to send 1,100 medical personnel to help people affected by Hurricane Katrina in New Orleans and elsewhere in US South, September 2005. Washington refused the offer.

of Cuban internationalists who served in Angola were Gerardo Hernández, Fernando González, and René González. Together with Antonio Guerrero and Ramón Labañino, they are today known around the world as the Cuban Five—Cuban revolutionaries who were arrested and framed by the US government and have been doing hard-time in US prisons since 1998. They are being held hostage to the refusal of the Cuban people to surrender to Washington's fifty year-old demand to return to the imperialist-dominated fold.

René served in a tank battalion in Cabinda in 1977–78. It was an experience that he said "taught me that the most beautiful things are accomplished by human beings who are imperfect, each of us giving history a little shove."

Fernando was stationed in southern Angola in the decisive years 1987–89, when Cuban and Angolan troops defeated the South African invaders at the battle of Cuito Cuanavale. He was assigned to the Information Section of the Southern Troops Group, processing the intelligence reports coming in from the front lines.

Gerardo led a reconnaissance platoon in Cabinda in 1989–90. "Angola was a school" for all the Cuban internationalists, including himself, he wrote in a letter from prison.[6]

Aren't the three of them representative of the hundreds of thousands of Cubans who took part in that historic internationalist mission?

ZAYAS: The courage and integrity shown by the Five is an example to millions around the world. It's a manifestation of the same internationalism the Cuban people—including Fernando, Gerardo, and René—demonstrated in Angola. They are an example of the type of men and women produced by Cuba's socialist revolution.

The five of them were trying to stop the United States from using US-based Cuban terrorists to carry out bombings and other actions against the Cuban people. They put themselves at risk in order to defend the revolution. They've served more than twelve years in prison, but they haven't been beaten down. They know that what they did was just, that they should not be in prison. They continue to express their convictions and fight for their freedom. That is why they are considered heroes here in Cuba, and justly so.

Because of their conduct behind prison walls, more and more people in the world know that what is being done to them is criminal. They have carried their struggle to the world, and the US government is paying a political price for their continued imprisonment.

They're showing what the Cuban Revolution is. And they *will* return, of that we can be sure.

WATERS: The experience of Angola—to have stayed with this internationalist commitment for almost sixteen years—had a broad impact on the political consciousness of the Cuban people. Fidel once said the revolutionary spirit of voluntary labor—something both he and Che had championed during the opening years of the revolution, but had sharply declined in the 1970s and early 1980s—sought refuge during that period in defense, in the mobilization of the Territorial Troop Militia, in the work of the internationalist missions. The rectification process of the late 1980s, which included the revival of voluntary work brigades to build homes, schools, child care centers, and clinics, and then the class solidarity that enabled Cuban working people to confront and surmount the political and economic challenges to the revolution in the wake of the implosion of the Soviet Union—all that would have been impossible without the internationalism, without the experience of Angola.

ZAYAS: We often talk about how we've provided help to other peoples on these missions. We go to help, to teach, to collaborate.

But Cubans have also learned a great deal. Like the way doctors in Cuba are now being trained—at the side of the patient. A doctor who trains at the patient's side is really trained. It's different from the training one gets in a classroom with a video. It used to be said here that doctors really start to understand what medicine is only when they finish their studies and begin to have patients. Today we take the student to the patient beginning in their first or second year. That's a completely different kind of training. And it's a product, in part, of what we learned from our internationalist missions.

Those serving on internationalist missions have received something else. Today's generation didn't

---

6. See pp. 107–19 for accounts by René González, Fernando González, and Gerardo Hernández of their experience in Angola.

live in the Cuba of old. They see photographs of what Cuba was like then, but they don't know how life was under capitalism. It's not that there are no problems in Cuba today. But when young Cubans go on internationalist missions, they see the reality in these places firsthand, and that gives them a clearer understanding of what the revolution changed in Cuba.

Look at what's happening in Venezuela now. Don't think that the Cubans serving in Venezuela today are just helping the Venezuelans. They're also learning what life is like in a country that hasn't had five decades of socialist revolution, with a leadership like Cuba has had, which has educated the Cuban people.

Then there's the help we've given to countries facing big catastrophes—hurricanes, floods, earthquakes. Cuban doctors have gone places where people have never seen a doctor, where they may have just enough food to survive but die from lack of basic medical attention. For everyone who has gone on these missions, that kind of experience is extremely important. It creates a consciousness different from what they had before.

They go places where even news doesn't arrive, because there are no means of communication, neither radio nor television. Simple survival is the aim. Living that reality helps mold our consciousness.

Cuban volunteers on internationalist missions in other countries are learning what Cuba used to be like. They're living in the world where such conditions still exist. They're learning about capitalism, about the exploitation of man by man.

So it's not only about helping. We also receive.

PART IV

The Cuban Five in Angola—In their own words

THE CUBAN FIVE—WHO THEY ARE

Gerardo Hernández, Ramón Labañino, Antonio Guerrero, Fernando González and René González are Cuban revolutionaries who during the 1990s volunteered to gather information for the Cuban government on the activities of Cuban-American counterrevolutionary groups based in southern Florida. These paramilitary outfits, operating on US soil with virtual impunity, have a long record of carrying out bombings, assassinations and other deadly attacks against targets in Cuba as well as supporters of the Cuban Revolution in the United States, Puerto Rico and elsewhere.

On September 12, 1998, the five were arrested by the FBI. They were framed up and convicted on more than thirty charges, which included acting as unregistered agents of the Cuban government, possession of false identity documents, and "conspiracy to gather and transmit national defense information"—i.e., conspiracy to commit espionage.

They were given sentences ranging from fifteen years for René González to double life plus fifteen years for Gerardo Hernández. Despite a growing worldwide campaign to win their freedom, they have now spent more than fourteen years in captivity—hostages to Washington's demand that the people of Cuba abandon their socialist course. Their story is told in *The Cuban Five: Who They Are, Why They Were Framed, Why They Should be Free* by Martín Koppel and Mary-Alice Waters.

BILL HACKWELL

Rally in Havana demands release of five Cuban revolutionaries from US prisons, May 1, 2010.

ANGOLA WAS A SCHOOL FOR EVERYONE
Mary-Alice Waters

When Gerardo Hernández Nordelo graduated from Cuba's Institute for Advanced Study of International Relations (ISRI) in 1989, like hundreds of thousands of other Cubans had done, he volunteered for duty in Angola. The Revolutionary Armed Forces of Cuba (FAR) was then engaged in the final stages of a nearly sixteen-year internationalist mission, fighting alongside the People's Armed Forces for the Liberation of Angola (FAPLA), to defend the government of that former Portuguese colony against the invading forces of the apartheid regime of South Africa and its imperialist-backed allies based in Zaire.

In 1989–90, Lieutenant Hernández led the Cuban-Angolan Scouting Platoon of twelve men attached to the Eleventh Tactical Group of the Tenth Tank Brigade, stationed in the Angolan province of Cabinda.

The following account of those years is by José Luis Palacio, a mechanic by trade and one of the men who served under Hernández in Cabinda. It was originally published under the title "Twelve Men and Two Cats" in March 2006 in *Guerrillero*, the provincial newspaper of Pinar del Río in western Cuba.

Palacio's tribute to the leadership qualities of Hernández—or simply "Gerardo" as he is known to millions around the world fighting for his freedom—goes far to explain why the US government has singled him out for especially brutal and vindictive treatment. Among the Cuban Five, Hernández was given the most draconian penalty of all—two life sentences plus fifteen years. He has been denied the right to receive visits from his wife, Adriana Pérez, since his 1998 arrest.

Hernández sent a photocopy of the *Guerrillero* article to Pathfinder Press after receiving a copy of *Malcolm X, Black Liberation, and the Road to Workers Power* by Jack Barnes. That book, published by Pathfinder Press, includes one of the photos on these pages—the picture of Hernández together with other members of his platoon around a cooking fire. The other two photos of the platoon reproduced here were mailed by Gerardo from the maximum-security Victorville penitentiary in California, where he is being held.

"Cuba sure hurts!"—Cartoon by Gerardo Hernández, 2003, drawn while in Victorville US Penitentiary, California.

Reprinted from *The Cuban Five: Who They Are, Why They Were Framed, Why They Should Be Free* (Pathfinder, 2012).

In accompanying letters, Hernández commented:

> It's been twenty years, but I remember as if it were today the moment when we took that photo around the fire in Angola. We were making a *dulce de coco* [a coconut dessert]. I remember everyone's names, including the two Angolan combatants in the picture, who were part of our scouting team.
>
> Several Cuban combatants from my platoon often write to me, including three members of what they called my "Matancera squad," since all of them were from Matanzas—José Ramón Zamora, Fidel Martell, and Wilfredo Pérez Corcho. All three are peasants, very modest people, and very revolutionary. They sent me these two photos, which I am now sharing with you.
>
> The quality of the originals is not very good due to the passage of time and the conditions under which they were developed and printed. . . .
>
> In the photo with the tank . . . standing on the ground is José Luis Palacio, from Pinar del Río. For some years I have kept an interview that Palacio gave to the newspaper in his province, which moved me very much when I read it. I'll look for it among my papers and send you a copy.
>
> I have great admiration for all those compañeros who volunteered for such a mission. At that time they were practically youngsters. I had been asked to give them classes in certain subjects, that is, I was supposed to teach them, but I was the one who wound up learning a lot from them. Angola was a great school for everyone.

The identifications in the captions were provided by Hernández. The comments in brackets in the interview that follows are his also.

TWELVE MEN AND TWO CATS
With Gerardo Hernández and his platoon in Angola

Zenia Regalado with José Luis Palacio
MARCH 2006

A Pinar del Río native was in Angola with Lieutenant Gerardo Hernández Nordelo. He remembers him as lively and jocular, always drawing cartoons of the soldiers in his reconnaissance platoon; reading Che's diary. The first to get up in the morning and the last to go to bed. Always very concerned with the health of the men under his command.

✧

When a group of twelve men have to sleep two and a half meters underground, shake off the homesickness that slowly eats at them with each delayed letter, march through snake-infested terrain, that's when friendship soars to its greatest heights.

So one can understand why José Luis Palacio Cuní would feel out of sorts when he returned from Angola in 1991 and why he would miss the down-to-earth camaraderie and kidding around by those platoon mates of the Tenth Tank Brigade in Cabinda.

At night they killed time playing seven-piece dominoes or playing cards. The latter was the favorite entertainment of Lieutenant Gerardo Hernández Nordelo, [Actually it was dominoes.—GH] who was good-humored and always roused them at 5:00 a.m. with that characteristic expression of his: "Stand up, soldiers! As straight as Cuba's palm trees!"

At that time nobody imagined that Gerardo—who shared the same hole with them—would become a hero, and that he would have to withstand even greater tests—nothing less than imprisonment in the United States.

None of Palacio's friends wanted to believe him that afternoon when they were watching television and, in the middle of a little party, this dark-skinned man who lives in the new twelve-story building at "Hermanos Cruz" told them, "Damn! That man in the photo was my leader in Angola. It's Lieutenant Nordelo!"

Two cats in the platoon

Palacio was in Angola, in Cabinda, for two years and three months. He had been working at the Machinery and Equipment Repair Enterprise, what was then the EREA, when he was called to fulfill his duty as a reservist. It was 1989, and he left behind a daughter who was just a little over three years old.

How did you all adjust to sleeping in the dugout? was one of the first questions we asked in our interview.

"The dugouts were six meters long and two or three meters wide. It wasn't easy getting used to sleeping there, but when you know it's safer than having your body out in the open, you have to do it.

"I was the only Pinar del Río native among those twelve men. The majority were from Matanzas, and we also had some *orientales* [from eastern Cuba] and some from Havana. At night when we were down there, someone would start telling the others that the most beautiful place in Cuba was Viñales; then someone else would jump in talking about his province, and so on. . . .

"A young guy from Matanzas, as soon as he arrived, began to take care of two cats. Those little animals really were internationalist soldiers too, because there were mice underground, and while we slept we often heard the cats hunting. They were very attached to us.

"Our lieutenant completed his mission, and then Gerardo arrived, a graduate of the Institute for Advanced Study of International Relations. The head

---

Reprinted from *The Cuban Five* (Pathfinder, 2012).

of the Eleventh Tactical Group told us, 'This is your new commander.' I remember very well Nordelo's first words:

"'I'm going to share the happiness, the sadness, and all other emotions with you. I'll just be one of you, like a brother, simply another human being.' We liked him a lot from the start.

"At night he would talk about when he was at the university, about his life as a student, about his cartoons, about his mother and his wife.

"He was very funny and knew how to tell jokes. In class he would give us a six-minute break, and during that time he would draw cartoons of us and say, 'That's what you were like in class.'

"When he saw someone was sad, Gerardo would even show him his own letters. When you're so far away, nothing is worth more than someone writing you.

"We played baseball in our free time. Was he good? To tell the truth, no, he wasn't. He was a pitcher, and since we were playing for fun, it didn't matter much. . . .

"He set up a radio; he always had to be doing something. He wrote the communiqués and jokes that were read by a soldier."

El Corcho

The tall, slender, dark-skinned man recalled that in the platoon there was a very thin young man named Pérez Corcho, who they nicknamed "El Corcho" [The Cork].

Everyone would call to him, "El Corcho, come here" and "El Corcho, go there." When his birthday came along, Gerardo got the idea that we should celebrate it. He asked for permission, and it was granted.

For the occasion they made wine from rice and from pineapples, which were very abundant in the area. That day they didn't go to the unit's main mess hall. [It wasn't wine but a kind of fruit drink, because alcohol was prohibited. —GH]

Many of those in the group of twelve had no idea how to cook, but they invented things. Gerardo wrote some jokes for the occasion and a communiqué. He always combined happy themes with patriotic ones, says his former subordinate.

COURTESY GERARDO HERNÁNDEZ

Gerardo Hernández with members of scouting platoon in Cabinda, Angola, 1989–90. **Atop tank, from left:** Pembele, Angolan combatant; Adolfo, center front; Henry, center back; Hernández. **Standing in front:** José Luis Palacio, interviewed in this article.

And did you have a strategy for dealing with the snakes?

"There were lots of cobras there. We had orders to sleep with mosquito netting and to put one boot inside the other so as not to leave them a space they could slide into, since they always seek body warmth.

"Gerardo would be the last to go to bed and always told us, 'Stuff your boots together the way you now know how to.' He always paid attention to those details, even though he was very young.

"Every third or fourth day we marched forty or fifty kilometers [twenty-five or thirty miles] through the jungle on our reconnaissance missions. We went together in a platoon made up of Angolans from FAPLA and the Cubans.

"Once one of the Angolans discovered a six-meter-long boa and killed it. They had a lot of respect for boas and said that we Cubans didn't fear even those beasts, since we didn't kill them.

"Lieutenant Nordelo always alerted us to everything, and one of the things he stressed most was the need to respect our own families and the families that lived there.

"I had previously seen on television Angola's poverty and what the UNITA troops were doing, but none of that could compare with what I saw afterward. Children living in very bad conditions, living in those huts, skinny, emaciated, and I couldn't help comparing them to ours and thinking that sometimes we weren't really conscious of what we had.

"For me, Angola was a school. I learned to value life and internationalism more, and to give a little of myself.

"One of Gerardo's many good ideas was about the children of the place where we were. He asked people to make homemade toys for the children, even rag dolls. It was very nice."

When you saw Gerardo on TV, what did you feel?

"At first I was very sad, thinking of a man who was such a revolutionary, such a good comrade, who had been so concerned for all of us, and who was today imprisoned—in the United States.

"But now I see it differently. It makes me happy to remember that the lieutenant at whose side I spent so much time is today a symbol of patriotism, that he has not given in. He has withstood so much; they haven't even allowed him to see his wife. That man, who was taking care of all of us, has not been able to have children!

"At the same time, I feel more revolutionary and committed. I also hope he will return and that those twelve Cubans will be able to meet again to recall the times we lived through in Angola."

Palacio, a modest man, a party member, a refrigeration and air conditioning mechanic in a cold storage plant, has not written Gerardo because he didn't have the address of the prison. Nor does he seek the limelight in recounting his days together with that lieutenant who liked to read so much.

It was Palacio's friend Félix Peña, an official of the provincial committee of the party, who encouraged him to speak with a reporter—to share with many more people his experiences with that genu-

COURTESY GERARDO HERNÁNDEZ

Gerardo Hernández with Cuban and Angolan combatants in Angola making dulce de coco (a coconut dessert). "**First row, from left to right:** Aldolfo, Pembele (Angolan), Nelson Abreu, and Gabriel Basquito (Angolan). Behind them are Yoel and myself."—GH

ine Cuban, whose ideals support him as straight as the Cuban palms he talked about to his men, as if to remind them they were born in a small island accustomed to nobleness.

Hernández's scouting platoon was part of a tactical group belonging to the Tenth Tank Brigade in Cabinda, which took part in reconnaissance missions to protect Cuban units and troops.

When he gave classes to his soldiers, Palacio reports, Gerardo would stress to them the importance of sharpening their skills for observing the enemy in order to track them.

A scout looks for signs on the ground indicating where the adversary might be. He must study the makeup of the opposing army, its weaponry.

All members of that twelve-man platoon—a symbolic number in the history of Cuba—have a photo of the group. Gerardo himself took it. In different ways this patriot has things in common with Ignacio Agramonte, that fierce attorney, that man of letters and also of action in the fields of Cuba, capable of wielding a machete but also of writing tender lines to his wife.

And this Cuban hero, who has grown while locked up in a US prison cell, left for his wife Adriana, along with the song Dulce abismo [Sweet abyss] by Silvio Rodríguez, this poem by Roberto Fernández Retamar entitled "Filin"*:

> *If they tell me you have gone away*
> *And will not come back*
> *I won't believe it*
> *I will wait for you and wait for you.*
>
> *If they tell you I have gone*
> *And will not return*
> *Don't believe it*
> *Wait for me*
> *Always.*

---

* *Filin* (feeling) is a genre of Cuban popular music that developed in Havana during a period of growing social unrest in the 1940s and '50s, incorporating elements of both jazz and Cuban bolero.

Cuban Angolan platoon under command of Gerardo Hernández

Platoon attached to Eleventh Tactical Group, Tenth Tank Brigade, Cabinda, Angola, under command of Lieutenant Gerardo Hernández Nordelo, 1989–90. Starting with front row from left to right, Hernández wrote, are: "Wilfredo Pérez Corcho (with a cat), Fidel Martell (with the other cat), Palacio, Bouza, and Adolfo. (Bouza is from the Zapata Swamp area, and the last that I heard of him, he was an official of the municipal Cuban Communist Party in Soplillar.) I'm in the middle, and behind are Gabriel Basquito (Angolan), Henry, Manuel (who also graduated from the ISRI [Institute for Advanced Study of International Relations] and may now be a diplomat), José Ramón Zamora, two compañeros whose names unfortunately I cannot remember now, Nelson Abreu, another compañero (with the sunglasses) whose name I cannot recall, and Carlos Amores, with the camera, our current ambassador to Malaysia. For most of those whose names I cannot recall, it's because they were in the platoon for only a short time after I arrived because they completed their missions and returned to Cuba."

COURTESY GERARDO HERNÁNDEZ

I LEARNED MORE THAN FROM ALL THE BOOKS I STUDIED OR COULD HAVE STUDIED

Fernando González
DECEMBER 2012

"The two years I was in Angola, from 1987 to 1989, were a milestone in my life," wrote Fernando González. "They were of enormous importance for my development as a revolutionary and as a human being."

This is how Fernando González Llort summarized what it meant for him to have been part of the massive effort by the men and women of Cuba to help that African country defend its independence and sovereignty, newly won from Portugal, against South Africa's apartheid regime.

González wrote from his prison cell in Terre Haute, Indiana, in response to questions the *Militant* had asked him about his experiences as an internationalist combatant in Angola. He had been stationed in the southern part of the country during the final stage of the protracted war against the US-backed South African invaders.

'We left for Angola enthusiastically'
In the summer of 1987 González graduated with honors from Cuba's Higher Institute of International Relations (ISRI), which trains students for diplomatic service abroad.

"Part of the curriculum," he wrote, "was military training, including practical work in reconnaissance. I graduated with an academic degree and the rank of lieutenant in the reserves of the Revolutionary Armed Forces (FAR)." He was also an active member of the Union of Young Communists (UJC).

"Soon after finishing school almost our entire graduating class was called for active duty in the FAR. We all volunteered for internationalist missions in Angola and left enthusiastically.

"Cuban military collaboration in Angola, which had begun twelve years earlier, was by then legendary for its heroism and selfless internationalism," González continued. "It was hard to find a Cuban who didn't know someone who had carried out a mission and talked of the experiences they'd lived through there. It was an honor for a young revolutionary to go to Angola and to be part of that effort.

"A few members of my graduating class who, for health reasons, weren't allowed to join the group of us going to Angola appealed the decisions of the medical commission and fought to be accepted. They moved heaven and earth, and eventually were allowed to join.

"It's an example of the importance we gave to being part of the experience in Angola and the enthusiasm with which we welcomed the opportunity."

Battle of Cuito Cuanavale
Once in Angola, González wrote, "I spent the first six months in a unit stationed in the city of Lubango, in the south. There we received training in reconnaissance before we were assigned to different units. We were a relatively small group of about thirty-five, so all knew each other by name.

"During the time we were in Lubango, we read the intelligence reports about the events taking place in Cuito Cuanavale," he said.

Toward the end of 1987, the apartheid regime's forces launched a new invasion of Angola, backed by its allies, the Angolan counterrevolutionary group UNITA, based among the Ovimbundu people in the south. The invasion rapidly created a critical situation. Enemy forces encircled the town of Cuito Cuanavale in the southeast and threatened

---

Reprinted from the *Militant*, December 3, 2012.

to inflict a major defeat on the Angolan army, the People's Armed Forces for the Liberation of Angola (FAPLA). Cuba's revolutionary leadership responded to appeals from the Angolan government by massively reinforcing its Angolan mission. "We even ran the risk of weakening our own defenses," Cuban president Fidel Castro noted in 1991, "and we did so."*

For the first time since the opening months of the war in early 1976, Cuban troops swept south toward the Angola-Namibia border in a powerful flanking operation. Simultaneously they fought their way toward Cuito Cuanavale (see map on page 43).

By March 1988 the combined forces of Cuban volunteers, FAPLA troops, and Namibian liberation fighters had dealt the South African army a resounding defeat. The apartheid forces began retreating and sued for peace. A series of tripartite negotiating sessions, involving Angola, South Africa and Cuba, led to a December 1988 agreement, signed at the United Nations in New York. The South African government withdrew completely from Angola and ceded independence to Namibia. With Angola's independence assured, Cuban forces withdrew. The final units returned to Cuba between January and May 1991, ahead of the agreed-on schedule.

* See p. 77.

Cuban and Angolan soldiers on captured South African tank, March 1988, at Cuito Cuanavale, southern Angola, where invading force of white supremacist regime was dealt decisive defeat. Fernando González was stationed in south at that time.

"Around the fourth month of training," González recounted, "officers from general headquarters visited our unit and met with all the officers and soldiers there to explain in detail the decision of the FAR high command and the leadership of the revolution that our troops would advance toward the border with Namibia.

"We understood the strategic importance of moving our units to the south of Angola, and the decision the Commander in Chief [Fidel Castro] had made to send to Angola units with great combat experience, such as the 50th 'Baraguá' Division. Even with our limited knowledge of military questions, we saw the decisive character of this historic moment.

"At that time," González continued, "the southernmost line of Cuban troops was along an axis that went from the port of Namibe in the west, passed through Lubango, and ended at Menongue in the east. Cuito Cuanavale was a ways past Menongue.

"As we had not finished our training, we remained in the rearguard of the Cuban forces, in Lubango, when the Southern Troop Grouping (ATS) moved south and headed for Cahama, Tchipa, and other towns to occupy positions just a few kilometers from the border with Namibia."

Near the Namibian border

"When our training was over," González said, "a group of us were sent to ATS headquarters in Cahama, where we were assigned by the Intelligence Section to different locations. Most of our group continued on the next day to find their designated units. I remained in Cahama, in the Intelligence Section, where I served as an officer of the command post for three or four months. My responsibilities were twenty-four-hour shifts to process all the information sent by units in the field about reconnaissance carried out in their area, and to prepare a daily report about these activities, which was supplemented by the results of intelligence received by radio and electronic means."

After the defeat of the apartheid

114 MORE THAN FROM ALL THE BOOKS

forces at Cuito Cuanavale and the agreement to begin to withdraw Cuban troops, ATS headquarters was moved back to Lubango. González was transferred there and remained in Lubango for the rest of his mission in Angola.

"The leadership of the Intelligence Section assigned me to the Lubango Operations Group, where I served as liaison with FAPLA headquarters. My responsibility was to coordinate the exchange of information about the results of reconnaissance. Each day I would take the information obtained by our reconnaissance in southern Angola to the FAPLA headquarters. There, in the Intelligence section at their headquarters, this information was plotted on the map and we checked our information against each other's.

"I prepared daily reports for the ATS Intelligence Section in Cahama and reports for the commander of the Lubango Operations Group on enemy deployment. I also served as an intelligence adviser for the 31st Tactical Group, based on the outskirts of Lubango."

While he was serving in Lubango, González recounted, "UNITA forces detonated a bomb on the rail line connecting Namibe with Lubango. A firefight was also reported at one of our posts. We had troop detachments guarding the railroad at various points along the way. I was ordered to take command of a group of soldiers and go to the area where the attack took place to determine the needs of our comrades there."

Returning to Lubango, González said, "I joined the general staff of the ATS and participated as a translator in one of the meetings related to the tripartite negotiations between Angola, Cuba and South Africa."

Writing about this assignment, González commented, "I had studied English at ISRI. They put a lot of emphasis on languages there. But we were never trained as translators. Furthermore, the focus, at least back then, was not on communication so much as reading and expressing oneself verbally or in writing.

"I didn't participate as a translator because I was qualified to do it. It was a matter of necessity. In fact, after almost two years in Angola without practicing a language that I had learned only in school, my English was very rusty."

'Experience I draw on in prison'

Looking back on his experience in Angola, González said, "I learned a lot from the Cubans and Angolans around me. I learned from their spirit of camaraderie and solidarity under difficult conditions. From the modesty of so many. From the collective, team effort that prevailed despite cultural differences between the Cuban and Angolan combatants, and from the richness those very differences brought us. We learned from each other. Everyone felt a sense of responsibility

"At the time I was twenty-four, twenty-five years old. The majority of the Cuban soldiers were younger, and many of the Angolans I met were only sixteen or seventeen. During those two years I saw many Cubans who arrived in Angola as recruits with the physical and psychological traits of adolescents, and who transformed themselves into young men steeled by discipline and responsibility, with the capacity to confront difficulties, and with

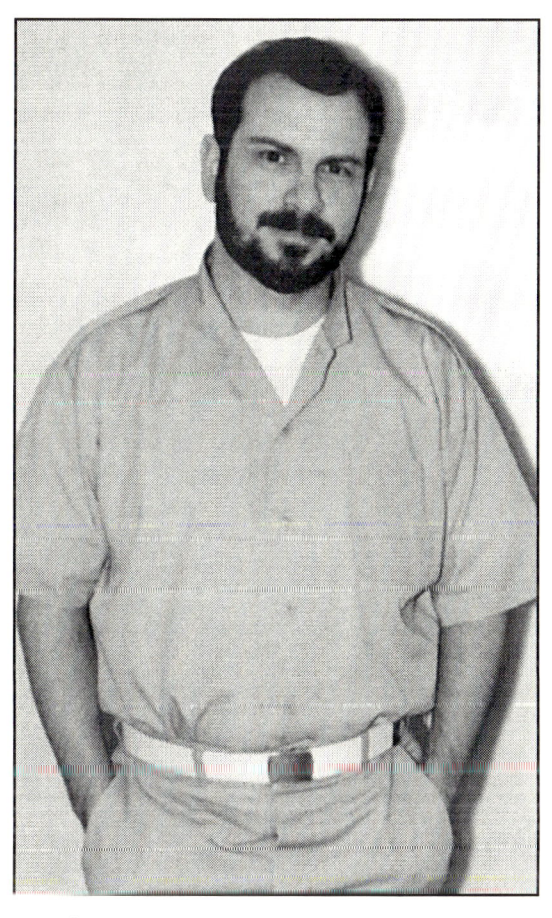

Drawing on experience in Angola, González says, has helped him "withstand conditions of prolonged imprisonment." **Above:** González at US prison in Terre Haute, Indiana. He is currently at federal prison in Safford, Arizona.

revolutionary consciousness.

"I myself was no stranger to this process of maturing under the impact of these conditions. I had barely graduated from the university. In Angola I learned—from both Angolans and Cubans—that no matter how much training you may have received, certain things are more important for a revolutionary: the development of character, sensitivity as a human being, a spirit of solidarity.

"I learned more by seeing with my own eyes the effects of colonialism, and its consequences for a people—in this case the Angolan people—than I did from all the books I had studied or could have studied.

"I saw the fighting spirit of that people and their determination to overcome the past, their efforts to repel foreign aggression and defeat the foreign-backed counterrevolutionaries.

"That was a lesson I always draw on. Including here, withstanding conditions of prolonged imprisonment.

"Although I didn't take part directly in combat I had the good fortune and feel proud to have been a member of the Southern Troop Grouping, especially during the decisive moments for the Cuban mission that led to the final victory."

While in Angola, González was taken into membership in the Cuban Communist Party. He was also awarded two medals for his service. After his return to Cuba, González was released from active duty and began graduate studies in international relations at ISRI.

A few years later he began a new internationalist mission. This time in the United States.

COURTESY FERNANDO GONZÁLEZ

Right: Fernando González in Angola. **Left:** González (center, seated) and other Cuban soldiers during moment of rest between military operations.

ANGOLA TAUGHT ME THAT THE MOST BEAUTIFUL WORKS ARE ACCOMPLISHED BY IMPERFECT MEN

René González
JUNE 2005

In 1977–79 René González took part in an internationalist combat mission in Angola. The following interview on his experience there was printed in the June 13, 2005, issue of the Cuban daily *Trabajadores.*

In the 2001 frame-up trial of the Cuban Five, González was convicted of charges of failure to register as a foreign agent and conspiracy to act as an unregistered foreign agent. In October 2011, after serving thirteen years in prison, he was placed on "supervised release" and remains under court order to serve that additional penalty in the United States.

When González mentions the crime in Barbados he is referring to the 1976 bombing of a Cuban airliner that killed all seventy-three aboard moments after taking off from the Barbados airport. The bombing was organized by CIA-trained Cuban counterrevolutionaries Luis Posada Carriles and Orlando Bosch.

In April 1974 the dictatorship in Portugal was overthrown in the "Carnation Revolution," a coup by young military officers that unleashed a mass popular upsurge.

❧

René González Sehwerert's youthful spirit and internationalist sentiment came together in his life as a soldier during Angola's war of liberation. Trabajadores *reveals the feelings and motivations that brought one of our antiterrorist heroes to the African continent.*

I don't know if in the mid-1970s I would have needed too many reasons for carrying out an internationalist mission. It was in the air. Che's legacy was germinating. The empire's crimes wounded Cubans' collective sensibility with each news story of new aggression or of the latest military dictatorship making its debut or by directly wounding our own flesh with crimes like the one in Barbados.

Under those circumstances, the Carnation Revolution shook the Portuguese colonial empire like a breath of fresh air and opened up the doors to sovereignty for parts of Africa with which we were joined through centuries of exploitation.

When once again they turned to crime with the support and complicity of those who today try to give us lessons about human rights—apartheid South Africa had attacked the beginnings of a nation just starting to crawl in Angola—the Cuban people shook with anger. Trembling with anger myself and thanks to the help of some officials I managed to be included in the unit of my regiment that was assigned to carry out a mission. That's how I joined a tank battalion, as a gunner in an

COURTESY RENÉ GONZÁLEZ

René González at age 21 in Angola, 1977.

Reprinted from *The Cuban Five* (Pathfinder, 2012).

artillery crew, a day after having finished my three years of General Military Service.

Two years in Cabinda

After two months of training, the T-34 Tank Battalion arrived on the coast of Cabinda in March 1977. Our unit did not participate in combat activities. The closest we came was participating in an encirclement operation, shortly before the end of our tour. By then the initial military enthusiasm of the young troops had been tempered by the imminence of returning home.

Our initial amazement seeing the lush African landscape was followed by contact with an unknown culture and way of life. I was struck by the nobility, humility, and lack of malice of the Angolans, whom centuries of misery and exploitation had not managed to turn into predators. The word of any one of those peasants was worth more than the constitutions of all of the 'superior' countries that had gone to 'civilize' that continent.

An experience that had a big impact on me was seeing the hunger in the faces and bodies of the children. The look on their faces made you shiver. Through some tacit and silent agreement, each one of our two hundred combatants agreed, from the first day, to give up a portion of their meager rations to feed a dozen children who would wait for us by the side of the road three times a day as we were taking food to a small group of troops deployed near their village.

There are two juxtaposed moments that will forever be etched in my memory: those happy faces returning to their village and witnessing how a neighboring family was making a small coffin.

My stay in Angola coincided with the battle for the ninth grade. In the absence of combat, this task was taken on with enthusiasm; rustic classrooms were built in each company's area. I'm grateful for this task for reconnecting me with what I had learned in studying mathematics, which I was able to teach others. I had the pleasure of seeing a group of officers and soldiers return to the homeland with certificates showing the grade level they had conquered.

After two years of vigilance and intense preparation for combat, in March 1979 the last members of the T-34 Battalion of the Motorized Infantry Regiment of Cabinda boarded the ships that returned us to Cuba, with the satisfaction of having done our job and gone through a unique experience.

On the Zende hillock we left behind a renewed unit and a mountain of life experiences.

I never imagined that another experience—like the one I'm living now—would be able to go beyond the intensity and weight of the Angolan one in my upbringing and my life. That's the value that I see in my two years in Cabinda.

The work of imperfect men

That internationalist mission was the realization of a longing that made me grow as a human being. It wasn't all rose-colored. I had positive and negative experiences under difficult conditions. There I lived moments of tremendous joy and others of profound sadness; camaraderie was mixed with conflicts, I disagreed and I was in agreement, I got along with some and not with others, I made good friends or, simply, compañeros.

But each and every one of these experiences taught me something new and made me grow. I have gone back to that experience to resolve later problems, and each one of those combatants—perhaps like me at that moment without fully recognizing it—was a part of something much bigger than any one of us or even of our battalion.

The Angolan experience taught me that the most beautiful works are accomplished by imperfect men, each one of us a short impulse in history: that continual righting of wrongs that began with the first human injustice.

However, the role of Cuba in this epic poem was more than a short impulse. The push that the fight for Angola's sovereignty gave to the struggle against colonialism—that social cancer upon which opulence was built that today passes itself off as the civilized world—didn't stop until it reached the Cape of Good Hope, completely destroying the myth that was invented to enable them to carry out their policies of subjugation.

I think that it will be some time before humanity understands Cuba's altruism in Angola. In the individualistic world that is imposed on us, what someone has called 'sarcastic skepticism' corrodes and immobilizes the collective consciousness forged in the masses. It's a means of domination used by those who build their fortunes on them.

But history is already written, at least up to this point, and the epic deed of our people in Africa is part of that. As it will be when all of the peoples united as one have sunk the bourgeois empire, erasing, at last, hunger from the face of the last child who has suffered from it.

PART V

Operation Carlota

OPERATION CARLOTA

Gabriel García Márquez
1977

Written in 1977 by one of Latin America's best-known authors, "Operation Carlota" remains among the most complete accounts of the early years of the Cuban mission in Angola.

The United States first officially revealed the presence of Cuban troops in Angola in a November 1975 statement. At the time they estimated that fifteen thousand men had been sent. Three months later, during a brief visit to Caracas, Henry Kissinger said in private to President Carlos Andrés Pérez: "Our intelligence services must be slipping—we only found out that the Cubans were going to Angola when they were already there." On that occasion, however, he lowered his estimate to twelve thousand men sent from Cuba.

At that moment many Cuban soldiers, military specialists, and civilian technicians were in Angola, more than Henry Kissinger thought. There were so many Cuban ships anchored in Luanda Bay that President Agostinho Neto, counting them from his window, said, with a shudder of modesty characteristic of him, "It's not fair. At this rate Cuba will ruin itself," he told an official who was a friend of his.

The Cubans themselves had probably not anticipated that their aid in solidarity with the people of Angola would reach such proportions. But they clearly understood from the start that their support had to be rapid and decisive; they could leave no room for defeat.

Contacts between the Cuban Revolution and the MPLA (Popular Movement for the Liberation of Angola) had first been established in—and had remained at a level of great intensity since—August 1965, when Che Guevara was involved in the guerrilla column in the Congo. The following year, Agostinho Neto himself visited Cuba, accompanied by Endo, commander in chief of the MPLA, who would later be killed in battle. Both met with Fidel Castro. Later, because of the conditions of the struggle in Angola, those contacts became sporadic.

It wasn't until May 1975, as the Portuguese were preparing to leave their African colonies, that Cuban commander Flavio Bravo met Agostinho Neto in Brazzaville. Neto asked Bravo for help in transporting an arms shipment and consulted him on the possibility of receiving broader and more specific forms of aid. As a result of this meeting, Commander Raúl Díaz Argüelles went to Luanda three months later, at the head of a delegation of Cuban civilians. This time Agostinho Neto was more precise but not more ambitious; he asked for a group of Cuban instructors to set up and lead four military training centers.

Even a superficial knowledge of the situation in Angola was enough to see that Neto's request was typical of his modesty. The MPLA was founded in 1956. It was the oldest liberation movement in Angola and the only one with a broad popular base and a social, political, and economic program that addressed the conditions of the country. At the same time, however, it was the organization in the least favorable military situation. It had weapons from the Soviet Union but no forces trained to use them. On the other hand, regular troops of the army of Zaire—a force that was well trained and equipped—had been operating in

---

Published in *Por la libre: Obra periodística 4 (1974–1995)* [Freelance: Essays and articles 4 (1974–1995)]. Copyright © 1974, 1995 by Gabriel García Márquez. Reprinted by permission of the author.

Angola since March 25. In Carmona [Uíge] they had proclaimed a de facto government headed by Holden Roberto, leader of the FNLA (National Front for the Liberation of Angola) and Mobutu's brother-in-law. Roberto's links with the CIA were common knowledge.

Meanwhile, in the east, under the protection of Zambia, UNITA (National Union for the Total Independence of Angola) was operating under the leadership of Jonas Savimbi, an unprincipled adventurer who had long collaborated with the Portuguese military and foreign mining companies. To top things off, on August 5, 1975, South African troops crossed Angola's southern border from its occupied territory of Namibia, under the pretext of protecting the Ruacaná-Calueque hydroelectric complex.

All those forces with their enormous economic and military resources were ready to close in on Luanda. They planned to encircle it tightly on the eve of November 11, when the Portuguese army would abandon that vast, rich, beautiful territory where it had been so happy for five hundred years. So when the Cuban leaders heard Neto's request, they didn't limit themselves to a strict interpretation of its terms. Instead, they decided immediately to send a contingent of four hundred eighty specialists, who in a period of six months would set up four training centers and organize sixteen infantry battalions. They also sent twenty-five mortar batteries, antiaircraft machine guns, a team of doctors, one hundred fifteen vehicles, and communications equipment.

That first contingent was transported in three improvised ships. *Heroic Vietnam*, the only passenger ship used, had been bought by dictator Fulgencio Batista from a Dutch company in 1956 and converted into a school ship. The other two, *Coral Island* and *La Plata*, were merchant vessels outfitted on an emergency basis. The way they were loaded is a good illustration of the foresight and audacity with which the Cubans met their commitment to Angola.

It seems incredible that the Cubans brought with them their own fuel for their vehicles. Angola is an oil producer, while the Cubans have to ship their own fuel halfway across the world from the Soviet Union. The Cubans, however, preferred to take no risks, and on that very first voyage they took a thousand barrels of gasoline divided among the three ships. *Heroic Vietnam* carried two hundred tons in fifty-five-gallon tanks; it had to sail with its holds open to vent the fumes. *La Plata* carried the gasoline on deck. The night the Cubans finished loading the ships coincided with a popular Cuban festival celebrated with spectacular fireworks right from the docks of Havana, where a spark could have turned those three floating arsenals to ashes.

Fidel Castro himself came to see the ships off, as he would do with all the contingents that went to Angola. After seeing the conditions in which they would travel, he uttered a phrase typical of his spontaneity: "In any case," he said, "you'll be more comfortable than the *Granma* expeditionaries were on their trip."

There was no guarantee that the Portuguese military would let the Cuban instructors land. On July 26, 1975, when Cuba had received the MPLA's first request for aid, Fidel Castro asked Colonel Otelo Saraiva de Carvalho, then in Havana, to obtain permission from the Portuguese government for Cuba to send aid to Angola. Saraiva de Carvalho promised he would, but no reply had arrived. *Heroic Vietnam* reached Porto Amboim on October 4 at 6:30 a.m., *Coral Island* followed on October 7, and *La Plata* arrived October 11 at Pointe-Noire. They docked without authorization from anyone, but also without any opposition.

The Cuban instructors were received as planned by the MPLA and immediately opened the four training schools. One was in N'Dalatando, which the Portuguese called Salazar, three hundred kilo-

Heroic Vietnam, Cuban passenger ship used in late 1975 to transport troops and equipment as part of Cuba's response to urgent appeal from MPLA to repulse South African invaders advancing on Luanda.

meters east of Luanda. Another was in the Atlantic port city of Benguela. A third was in Saurimo, formerly Enrique de Carvalho, in the remote eastern desert province of Lunda, where the Portuguese had a military base they destroyed before withdrawing. The fourth was in the Cabinda enclave. By then, Holden Roberto's forces were so close to Luanda that a Cuban artillery instructor, giving his first lesson to the students at N'Dalatando, could actually see the mercenaries' armored vehicles advancing toward them.

On October 23 a mechanized brigade of South African troops invaded Angola from Namibia. Within three days they had taken, without resistance, the cities of Sa de Bandeira and Moçamedes. They treated it like a Sunday walk in the park. The South Africans had cassette players with dance music in their tanks. In the north, the leader of a mercenary column directed operations from a Honda sports car, sitting next to a blonde film actress. They advanced as if they were on vacation and sent out no advance patrols. He probably never knew from which direction the rocket came that blew his car to bits. The woman's travel bag contained only an evening dress, a bikini, and a printed invitation for the victory party that Holden Roberto had already planned to hold in Luanda.

By the end of that week, the South Africans had advanced more than six hundred kilometers into Angola, moving toward Luanda some seventy kilometers a day. On November 3 they attacked the few soldiers at the training center for recruits in Benguela. The Cuban instructors had to abandon the school to fight the invaders alongside their soldier trainees, and they could be heard resuming classes with them during pauses in the battle. Even the Cuban doctors had to recall their militia training and take to the trenches. The MPLA leaders had been prepared for guerrilla warfare but not full-scale battle. Now, however, they understood that only through an urgent appeal for international solidarity could they defeat the joint attack mounted by their neighboring states, backed by imperialism's most rapacious and destructive resources.

Internationalism is part of Cuba's heritage. The revolution has promoted and strengthened it in accordance with the principles of Marxism, but its essence was already well established in the deeds and writings of José Martí. That course of action has been demonstrated—and has been a source of conflict—in Latin America, Africa, and Asia.

In Algeria, even before the Cuban Revolution declared its socialist character, Cuba had already given considerable aid to the combatants of the FLN (National Liberation Front) in their war against French colonial rule—to the point that the government of General de Gaulle retaliated by banning Cubana de Aviación flights over France. Later, while Cuba was being devastated by Hurricane Flora [in 1963], a battalion of Cuban internationalist combatants went to defend Algeria against Morocco.[1]

In fact, there is no African liberation movement that has been denied Cuban solidarity, whether in the form of matériel, weapons, or the training of military and civilian technicians and specialists. Mozambique (since 1963), Guinea-Bissau (since 1965), Cameroon, and Sierra Leone have all, at one time or another, asked for and received Cuban solidarity and assistance. Sékou Touré, president of the Republic of Guinea, routed a mercenary landing with the help of a Cuban unit. Commander Pedro Rodríguez Peralta, today a member of the Central Committee of the Cuban Communist Party, was captured and imprisoned for several years by the Portuguese in Guinea-Bissau.

When Agostinho Neto called on Angolan students in Portugal to go study in the socialist countries, many of them were received by Cuba. At present, all of them are helping to build socialism in Angola, some with responsibilities of great importance. This is the case of Minga, an economist and currently Angola's finance minister; Enrique dos Santos, a geologist, commander, and member of the MPLA Central Committee, who is married to a Cuban; Mantos, an agronomist and present head of the Military Academy; and N'Dalu, who as a student was the best soccer player in Cuba; today he is the second in command of the First Brigade of Angola.

Nothing, however, better illustrates the duration and intensity of Cuba's presence in Africa than the fact that Che Guevara himself, at the height of his fame and in the prime of his life, went to fight alongside the guerrillas in the Congo. He left Cuba

---

1. See footnote, page 52.

on April 1, 1965, on the same date as his farewell letter to Fidel Castro in which he resigned his rank of commander and ended all legal ties to the Cuban government. He left alone, on a commercial airliner, under a false name and passport, with his physical appearance only slightly altered by two master strokes, and carrying a briefcase with works of literature and inhalers for his unrelenting asthma. He would spend dead time in hotel rooms playing interminable games of solitary chess. Three months later, he met up in the Congo with two hundred Cuban combatants who had come from Havana in a ship loaded with weapons.[2]

Che's specific mission was to train guerrillas for the National Council of the Revolution of the Congo, which was fighting Moise Tshombe, a puppet of Belgium's former colonial settlers and the international mining companies. Patrice Lumumba had already been murdered. The formal head of the National Council of the Revolution was Gaston Soumialot, but the person who actually directed military operations was Laurent Kabila, from his hideaway in Kigoma on the opposite shore of Lake Tanganyika. That undoubtedly helped preserve the real identity of Guevara, who, for greater security, did not appear to be the central leader of the Cuban mission. That's why he was known by the nom de guerre of Tatu, which means "Number Three" in Swahili.

Che Guevara remained in the Congo from April to December 1965. He not only trained guerrillas but led them in combat and fought alongside them. His personal ties with Fidel Castro, the subject of so much speculation, never weakened at any time. They maintained constant and cordial contact through very effective means of communication.

When Moise Tshombe was overthrown, the Congolese asked the Cubans to withdraw in order to make it easier to conclude an armistice. Che

First Cuban battalion sent to Angola in November 1975 was transported on Cubana Airlines flights in Bristol Britannia turboprops like this one.

Guevara left as he had arrived, silently. He flew from the airport in Dar es Salaam, the capital of Tanzania, on a commercial airliner. He buried his head in a book on chess problems, reading it from cover to cover to keep his face hidden during the six-hour flight. In the next seat, his Cuban aide tried to entertain the political commissioner of the Zanzibar army, an old admirer of Che's who spoke of him constantly throughout the flight, trying to obtain news of him and reiterating his desire to meet him again.

During his brief and anonymous passage through Africa, Che Guevara planted a seed that no one would be able to destroy. Some of his men went on to Brazzaville to train guerrilla units for the PAIGC,[3] led by Amilcar Cabral, and especially for the MPLA.

One of the columns they trained entered Angola clandestinely through Kinshasa and joined the struggle against the Portuguese under the name of the Camilo Cienfuegos Column. Another infiltrated into Cabinda and later crossed the Congo River to establish itself in Bengo, the province where Agostinho Neto was born and where a struggle against Portuguese rule had been waged for five centuries.

In other words Cuba's solidarity with Angola was not an impulsive or accidental action; it was the consequence of the Cuban Revolution's long-standing policy toward Africa. This time, however,

---

2. Little information about the Congo operation was publicly available before 1999, when Guevara's *Episodes of the Revolutionary War—Congo* was published. Guevara flew from Havana to Tanzania with Víctor Dreke, who was second in command of the column, and José María Martínez Tamayo (Papi), a member of Che's escort and his liaison with revolutionary forces in Latin America. The column was composed of 128 combatants, most of whom traveled to Tanzania by air. Che and the first volunteers arrived in the Congo April 24, 1965. See *From the Escambray to the Congo* by Víctor Dreke (Pathfinder, 2002).

3. The African Party for the Independence of Guinea and Cape Verde (PAIGC) took up arms against Portuguese rule in 1963. It won Guinea-Bissau's independence in 1974 and Cape Verde's in 1975.

a new and extraordinary element entered into the making of that delicate decision. It was no longer just a matter of sending all possible aid. At stake now was a large-scale regular war ten thousand kilometers away—a war whose economic and political costs could not be calculated, whose political consequences could not be predicted.

There was a possibility that the United States would intervene openly—not through mercenaries or through South Africa, as they had done until then; this was, without doubt, one of the troublesome unknowns. But a rapid analysis showed that the US would at least think several times about making such a move. It had just emerged from the Vietnam quagmire and the Watergate scandal. It had a president no one had elected.[4] Congress was attacking the CIA, which was losing prestige in public opinion. The US had to be careful not to openly appear as an ally of racist South Africa, either in the eyes of the majority of the African countries or in the eyes of the black population in the United States. It was also in the middle of a presidential election campaign and the year of the Bicentennial was about to begin. The Cubans, on the other hand, were certain to receive solidarity and material aid from the Soviet Union and other socialist countries. But the Cubans were also aware of the implications their action could have for the policy of peaceful coexistence and international détente.

It was a decision with irreversible consequences, a problem too big and too complex to be solved in twenty-four hours. But the leadership of the Cuban Communist Party had no more than twenty-four hours to make the decision, which it did, without vacillation, on November 5, during a long and calm meeting. Contrary to what has so often been said, the decision was an independent and sovereign act of Cuba. It was only after it was made, not before, that Cuba notified the Soviet Union.

On another November 5, this one in 1843, a slave called Black Carlota, from the Triunvirato sugar mill in the Matanzas region, had risen up, machete in hand, at the head of a slave rebellion and had been killed in the uprising. In homage to her, Cuba's action of solidarity in Angola was named Operation Carlota.

Operation Carlota began with the dispatch of a reinforced battalion of special forces comprised of six hundred fifty men. They were transported by plane in thirteen days of successive flights from the military section of the José Martí airport in Havana directly to Luanda airport, at the time still occupied by Portuguese troops. Their mission was to halt the offensive and keep the capital of Angola from falling into the hands of the enemy before the departure of the Portuguese. Then they were to keep up resistance until the arrival of reinforcements by sea. The men sent on the first two flights were convinced it was too late and hoped only to save Cabinda.

The first contingent left November 7, at 4:00 p.m., on a special Cubana flight. They flew in one of the legendary Bristol Britannia BB 218 turboprops, a plane that had been discontinued by its British manufacturer and retired from every other fleet in the world. The passengers remember that they numbered eighty-two, because it was the same as the number of expeditionaries who had sailed on the *Granma*. Wearing summer sportswear with no military insignia and traveling with briefcases and normal passports in their real names, they had the healthy appearance of tourists tanned by the Caribbean sun. The special forces battalion was part of the Ministry of the Interior, not the Revolutionary Armed Forces. Its members were skilled combatants, with a considerable grasp of ideology and politics. Some had university degrees. They read a great deal and were always seeking to increase their knowledge.

So the fiction of being civilians on a vacation must not have been so difficult to keep up. But their briefcases held machine guns. And the plane's cargo compartment had no luggage. Instead it was packed with light artillery, the combatants' individual weapons, three 75 mm cannons, and three 82-mm mortars. The plane was staffed by two flight attendants. The only change that had been made to it was the installation of a hatch in the floor so that weapons could be reached through the passenger cabin in case of emergency.

---

4 As US ruling-class divisions known as the Watergate Scandal deepened, president Richard Nixon resigned in August 1974 rather than face almost certain removal from office in impeachment proceedings already under way in the US Congress. Vice President Gerald Ford was sworn in as president. He ran for president two years later and lost to James Carter in 1976.

The flight from Havana to Luanda made a stopover in Barbados to take on fuel, in the middle of a tropical storm, and another of five hours in Guinea-Bissau to wait for nightfall and then fly in secrecy to Brazzaville. The Cubans used those five hours for sleep—the worst they ever had. The airport warehouses were so full of mosquitos that the sheets on the cots were left stained with blood.

Mobutu, with his proverbial arrogance, had once said that Brazzaville is lit up by the glow of Kinshasa, the dazzling modern capital of Zaire. And he was not wrong. The two cities face each other across the Congo River. Their airports are so close to each other that the first Cuban pilots had to study the maps well so as not to land on the enemy's runway. They managed to land without problems, with their lights off to avoid being seen from the other shore, and stayed in Brazzaville just long enough to get information by radio on the situation in Angola. Angolan commander Xieto, who had good relations with the Portuguese commissioner, had obtained authorization from him for the Cubans to land in Luanda.

The plane landed at 10 p.m. on November 8, with no assistance from the tower and in a torrential downpour. The second plane landed fifteen minutes later. Leaving Cuba at that very moment were three ships carrying an artillery regiment, a battalion of motorized troops, and crews for the mobile multiple rocket launchers, who would begin to land in Angola November 27. Meanwhile, Holden Roberto's columns were so close that, just hours before, in an attempt to hit the Gran Farni Fortress, where the Cubans were now gathered, one of their shells had killed an elderly Angolan woman. So the Cubans had no time to rest. They put on their olive-green uniforms, joined ranks with the MPLA soldiers, and marched off to battle.

For security reasons, the Cuban press did not publish news of the country's involvement in Angola. But, as often happens in Cuba, even with military matters as delicate as this, the operation was a secret zealously guarded by eight million people. The First Congress of the Communist Party, which was to be held a few weeks later and which became something of a national obsession throughout the year, took on a new dimension.

Volunteer units were organized by delivering notices privately to members of the first reserve units, which include all males between seventeen and twenty-five years of age and all former members of the Revolutionary Armed Forces. They were called in by telegram to their respective military committees, with no mention of why they were being summoned. The reason was so obvious, however, that everyone who considered he had some military capability reported to his committee without waiting for a telegram. It took a lot of work to keep that massive request to serve in the mission from turning into a national riot.

The process of selection was as strict as the urgency of the situation allowed. Military qualifications and physical and moral conditions were taken into account, but so too were work history and political education. Despite this rigor, there were countless cases of volunteers who managed to slip through the selective filters. There was the case of a highly skilled engineer who said he was a truck driver, a high official who successfully passed himself off as a mechanic, and a woman who was almost accepted as a rank-and-file soldier. There is also the case of the young man who went without his father's permission only to meet him later in Angola, since the father too had volunteered without telling his family. On the other hand, there was the twenty-year-old sergeant who, despite his efforts, was turned down and had to endure a blow to his machismo when his mother, a journalist, and his fiancée, a doctor, were selected to go to Angola. Some common criminals in prison also asked to be sent, but none of them were even considered.

The first woman to go, in early December, had been turned down several times with the argument that "this would be too hard for a woman." She was all set to go as a stowaway on a ship and had already hidden her clothes in the hold with the help of a photographer she knew, when she found out she had finally been chosen to go legally, and by plane. Her name is Esther Lilia Díaz Rodríguez. She is a twenty-three-year-old former schoolteacher who joined the armed forces in 1969 and was noted for her marksmanship during infantry training. With her, but separately, went three of her brothers: César, Rubén, and Erineldo. Each one individually, without letting the others know, had told his mother the same story: he was going off to the military maneuvers in Camagüey held in connection with the party congress. All returned safe and sound, and their mother is very proud that they went to Angola. But she still hasn't forgiven them for lying about the maneuvers in Camagüey.

Conversations with those who returned show that some went for very different personal reasons. At least one person went in order to desert; he later hijacked a Portuguese plane and asked for asylum in Lisbon. No one went against his will. Before leaving everyone had to sign a statement that they were volunteers. Some declined to go after having been chosen and had to face all kinds of public jokes and private scorn. But there's no doubt that the immense majority went to Angola with the full conviction that they were carrying out an act of political solidarity. They went with the same consciousness and courage they had displayed fifteen years earlier when they defeated the Bay of Pigs invasion at Playa Girón. Operation Carlota was not simply an expedition of professional soldiers; it was a war of the people.

Carried out over the course of nine months, the mobilization of human and material resources constituted a bold feat of epic proportions. The decrepit Britannias, patched up with brakes from Soviet Ilyushin 18s, kept up a constant and almost unbelievable airlift. Although their maximum load is normally 185,000 pounds, they often took off weighing 194,000 pounds, a figure that's off the charts. The pilots, normally limited to seventy-five hours a month, often flew more than two hundred.

In general, each of the three Britannias in service carried two full crews who rotated during the flight. But one pilot recalls being in his seat up to fifty hours on a round-trip flight, with forty-three hours of actual flying time. "There are moments," he said, with no pretense to heroism, "when you can't possibly get more tired than you already are." Under those conditions, and because of the differences in time zones, the pilots and flight attendants lost all track of time. Their only guide was the needs of their bodies—they ate when they were hungry and slept when they were tired.

The route from Havana to Luanda is bleak and desolate. At the Britannia's low cruising altitude—between eighteen thousand and twenty thousand feet—information on winds is nonexistent in today's era of the jet. The pilots took off in every direction without knowing the conditions of the route, flew at inadvisable altitudes to economize on fuel, and never had the slightest idea of what landing conditions would be. On the most dangerous stretch, between Brazzaville and Luanda, there was no alternate airport. In addition, the soldiers flew with loaded weapons and, in order to reduce weight, explosives were shipped without crates, missiles without outer protection.

The United States took aim at the Britannias' weakest point: their lack of range. When the government of Barbados was persuaded to stop the fueling stopovers, the Cubans established a transatlantic route from Holguín, in eastern Cuba, to Sal Island in Cape Verde. It was a daring trapeze act with no safety net. On the outgoing flight the planes would arrive with fuel for only two more hours, and on the return, flying against the wind, they would arrive with fuel for only one more hour. That dangerous route, too, was dropped to avoid causing trouble for defenseless Cape Verde. The cabins were then adapted to carry four additional tanks of fuel to allow the planes to fly nonstop, but with thirty fewer passengers, from Holguín to Brazzaville.

The other possible solution, stopping in Guyana, wouldn't work. First, the runway there was too short. Second, Texaco, which extracts Guyana's oil, refused to sell Cuba the fuel. Cuba tried to solve this problem by sending a ship loaded with gasoline to Guyana, but, because of an accident that seems hard to understand, the fuel was contaminated with dirt and water. In face of so many bitter difficulties, the Guyanese government remained firmly in solidarity with the Cubans, despite the fact that the US ambassador personally threatened the bombing and destruction of the Georgetown airport.

Planes were serviced in less than half the normal time. One pilot recalls that he flew several times without radar, but no one recalls an actual instrument failure. In those incredible conditions, 101 flights were made from the beginning to the end of the war.

Maritime transport was no less hazardous. Cuba's last two passenger ships, four thousand tons each, were fitted out with cots in all free spaces; latrines were set up in the nightclubs, bars, and corridors. Normal capacity, two hundred twenty-six passengers, was tripled on some voyages. Cargo ships, with a capacity for eighty crew members and others, began to sail with as many as a thousand passengers in addition to armored cars, weapons, and explosives. Field kitchens were set up in the cargo holds and lounges. To economize on water, disposable plates were used and plastic yogurt containers served as glasses. Ballast tanks were used for bathing and some fifty latrines that flushed overboard into the sea were set up on the decks.

The tired engines of the old ships began to break down after six months of such exceptional performance. This was the only cause for exasperation on the part of the first group to return home. Their much-awaited trip was delayed for several days because the filters on the *Heroic Vietnam* were clogged. When other ships in the convoy had to wait for it, some of the passengers came to understand Che Guevara's statement that the advance of a guerrilla unit is determined by the pace of the slowest man.

Those obstacles loomed large at the time, since Cuban ships were subjected to all sorts of provocation by US destroyers, which harassed them for days on end, and by US warplanes, which photographed them and flew over them at low altitudes.

Despite the difficult conditions of those trips, which lasted almost twenty days, no serious sanitary problems arose. In the forty-two voyages made during the six months of the war, the medical personnel onboard handled only one appendectomy, one hernia operation, and one outbreak of diarrhea caused by some canned meat. More difficult to contain was the epidemic of crew members who were determined to stay and fight in Angola. One of them, a reserve officer, somehow got hold of an olive-green uniform, disembarked mixed in with the troops as they landed, and managed to stay ashore. He became one of the best information officers of the war.

At the same time, Soviet material aid, arriving

"Angola in 1975 was a vast and wealthy country full of poverty," said Gabriel García Márquez. "The living standards of the local population were the lowest in the world, with an illiteracy rate of more than 90 percent." Cuban volunteer (right) teaching Angolan combatants to read and write.

through different channels, required a constant flow of skilled personnel to handle and teach others how to handle the new weapons and complex equipment still unfamiliar to the Angolans.

The chief of the Cuban general staff himself [Abelardo Colomé (Furry)] went to Angola at the end of November. Everything then seemed tolerable—except losing the war. Nevertheless, the historical truth is that it was about to be lost.

In the first week of December, the situation was so desperate that Cubans and Angolans were considering fortifying a position in Cabinda while establishing a beachhead around Luanda in order to begin evacuating the city. In addition, that somber prospect came at the worst possible moment for both Cubans and Angolans. The Cubans were preparing to hold the First Congress of the Communist Party December 17–24, and the leadership knew that a military defeat in Angola would be a mortal political blow. For their part, the Angolans were preparing for a conference of the OAU (Organization of African Unity) and wanted to go there with a military position more favorable for winning the support of the majority of African countries.

The adversities of December were due, in the first place, to the tremendous firepower of the enemy, who had received more than $50 million in military aid from the United States. In the second place, it was due to the delay with which Angola had asked for Cuban aid, and the inevitable time it took to transport the supplies. And finally, it was due to the conditions of poverty and cultural backwardness left in Angola by five hundred years of pitiless colonial rule. It was the last point, more than the other two, that created the greatest difficulties in the effort to fully integrate Cuban combatants with the armed population of Angola.

In reality, Cubans found in Angola the same climate as in their own country, the same vegetation, the same torrential rains, the same apocalyptic sunsets, the aroma of scrub brush and alligators. Some Cubans resembled Angolans so much that a joke soon made the rounds to the effect that it was possible to distinguish them only by touching the tip of their noses, because the Africans have soft nose cartilage from the way they were carried as babies, with their faces pressed against their mothers' backs.

The Portuguese colonial rulers were perhaps the most insatiable and cruelest in history. They built modern, beautiful cities designed so they could spend their entire lives in air-conditioned glass-walled buildings alongside stores with enormous neon signs. But these were cities for whites, like the ones the gringos had built around Old Havana, which the peasants looked at with astonishment when they first came down from the Sierra with rifles slung over their shoulders.

Beneath that shell of civilization was a vast and wealthy country full of poverty. The living standards of the native population were among the lowest in the world. The rate of illiteracy was more than 90 percent; cultural conditions as a whole were much like those of the Stone Age. In the cities of the interior only the men spoke Portuguese, and they kept as many as seven wives in the same house. Age-old superstitions obstructed not only everyday life but also the war. The Angolans had long been convinced that bullets could not harm a white man, they had a superstitious fear of airplanes, and they refused to fight in trenches because, they said, tombs were only for the dead.

In the Congo, Che Guevara had seen soldiers put on necklaces to protect themselves from artillery shells and bracelets to protect themselves from machine-gun fire. They would also sear their faces with smoldering embers to ward off the risks of war. Che became so interested in these cultural absurdities that he began a thorough study of African customs and learned to speak Swahili in an attempt to change them from within. He was aware that there was a deep, pernicious force planted in men's hearts that could not be defeated with bullets: the colonization of the mind.

Health care conditions, of course, were appalling. In San Pedro de Cota, the Cubans had to bring in a child for medical treatment almost by force. His entire body was burned from boiling water, and his family was simply waiting for him to die, believing he could not be saved. Cuban doctors also encountered diseases they had never even heard of. Under Portuguese rule, Angola had only ninety doctors for six million inhabitants, and most of the doctors were concentrated in the capital. When the Portuguese left, only thirty doctors stayed behind. On the very day he arrived in Porto Amboim, a Cuban pediatrician saw five children die for lack of medical supplies. That was an unbearable experience for a doctor, thirty-five years old, trained in a country with one of the lowest infant mortality rates in the world.

The MPLA had made great progress

EDITORA POLÍTICA

Raúl Díaz Argüelles (center, with sunglasses), first commanding officer of Cuban internationalist contingent, with some of first Cuban volunteers to arrive in Angola. Díaz Argüelles was killed during combat operations south of Luanda, December 1975.

against primitive thinking in its long and silent years of struggle against Portuguese rule, and had thus created the conditions for the final victory. In the liberated areas, they were raising the political and cultural level of the population, combating tribalism and racism, and providing free education and health care. They had sown the seeds of a new society.

Those extraordinary and praiseworthy efforts paled, however, when guerrilla warfare turned into a large-scale modern war and it became necessary to call on not only those with military and political training but the entire people of Angola. It was an atrocious war—one in which you had to be on the lookout for both mercenaries and snakes, cannons and cannibals. A Cuban commander, in the middle of a battle, fell into an elephant trap. Black Africans, conditioned by centuries of hatred for the Portuguese, were initially hostile to Cubans who were white. Many times, especially in Cabinda, Cuban scouts felt their presence betrayed by the primitive telegraph of the drums, which could be heard up to thirty-five kilometers away.

On the other side, the white South African soldiers would fire on ambulances with 140 mm cannon. On the battlefield they threw up smokescreens to pick up their dead who were white but left the dead who were black to the vultures. In the home of a UNITA minister who lived in the comfort appropriate to his rank, the men of the MPLA found in his refrigerator jars of entrails and bottles of frozen blood from the prisoners of war he had eaten.

Meanwhile, nothing but bad news reached Cuba. On December 11 in Hengo, where FAPLA forces were launching a major offensive against the South African invaders, an armored car with four Cuban commanders aboard ventured upon a path where sappers had previously detected mines. Although four cars had safely crossed the road before, the sappers had warned the Cubans not to take that route, since its only advantage was to gain a few minutes, at a time when there seemed to be no need for haste. The car had scarcely entered the track when it was blown into the air by an explosion. Two commanders of the battalion of special forces were seriously wounded. Raúl Díaz Argüelles, overall commander of operations in the internationalist mission in Angola, hero of the struggle against Batista, and a dearly loved figure in Cuba, was killed instantly. That was one of the most bitter pieces of news for the Cubans, but it was not the last in that long streak of bad luck.

The next day brought the disaster of Catofe, perhaps the biggest setback of the entire war. A South African column had repaired a bridge over the Nhia River with impressive speed. They had crossed the river under the cover of early-morning mist, and had caught the Cubans tactical rearguard by surprise. An analysis of this setback showed that it had been the result of an error by the Cubans. A European military officer with extensive experience in World War II considered that analysis too severe. He later told a high-ranking Cuban leader, "You don't know what an error in war is." But for the Cubans it was a very serious error, and just five days before the party congress.

Fidel Castro kept himself personally informed of the smallest details of the war. He saw off every ship, and before each departure gave a talk to the soldiers in the theater of La Cabaña. He personally picked up the commanders of the battalion of special forces who left in the first flight and drove them in his Soviet jeep to the foot of the stairway to the plane. During these sendoffs Fidel Castro must have had to repress a deep sentiment of envy for those going off to a war that he himself could not participate in. There wasn't a spot on the map of Angola that he couldn't identify, no feature of the terrain he hadn't memorized. His focus on the war was so intense and meticulous that he could quote any figure on Angola as if it were Cuba. He spoke of the cities, customs, and people of Angola as if he had lived there all his life.

At the beginning of the war, when the situation was urgent, Fidel Castro would spend up to fourteen hours straight in the command room of the general staff, at times without eating or sleeping, as if he were on the battlefield himself. He followed the details of every battle with colored pins on the detailed maps as big as the walls they covered, and remained in constant communication with the top command of the MPLA in a battlefield with a six-hour time difference.

In those uncertain days, some of his reactions revealed his confidence in victory. When an MPLA combat unit was forced to blow up a bridge to delay the advance of South African armored columns,

Fidel Castro sent them a message, suggesting: "Don't blow up any more bridges; you won't be able to pursue them later." And he was right. Only a few weeks later, brigades of Cuban and Angolan engineers had to repair thirteen bridges in twenty days to catch up with the invaders, then in flight.

On December 22, at the closing session of the party congress, Cuba officially announced for the first time that it had troops fighting in Angola. The outcome of the war continued to be uncertain. In his closing speech, Fidel Castro revealed that the invaders of Cabinda had been crushed in seventy-two hours; that on the northern front, Holden Roberto's troops, just twenty-five kilometers from Luanda on November 10, had been forced to retreat more than one hundred kilometers; and that the South African armored columns, which had advanced seven hundred kilometers in fewer than twenty days, had been stopped more than two hundred kilometers from Luanda and had not been able to continue their march. This was comforting and accurate news, but victory was still far off.

The Angolans had better luck January 12 when they went to the OAU conference in Addis Ababa. A few days earlier, troops under Cuban commander Victor Schueg Colás, an enormous and cordial black man who had been an auto mechanic before the revolution, drove Holden Roberto out of his illusory capital of Carmona, occupied the city, and a few hours later took the Negage military base.

At the beginning of January, aid from Cuba was so intense that fifteen Cuban ships were sailing simultaneously to Luanda. The irrepressible offensive of the MPLA on all fronts turned the tide once and for all. By mid-January, on the Southern Front, they were conducting offensive operations originally scheduled for April. South Africa was using Canberra planes and Zaire was flying Mirages and Fiats. Angola, on the other hand, had no air force, because the Portuguese had destroyed the bases before leaving. It had only a few old DC-3s that Cuban pilots had put back into service. At times those planes, used to carry the wounded, had to land at night on air strips lit with improvised lamps, and would arrive at their destination with vines and strands of jungle foliage wrapped around their wheels. At a certain point Angola had a fleet of MiG-17s flown by Cuban pilots, but they were considered the reserve of the top military command and were used only in defense of Luanda.

At the beginning of March, the northern front was liberated with the defeat of the British and American mercenaries the CIA had recruited in a last-ditch desperate effort. All the troops, and their full general staff, were concentrated in the south. The Benguela railroad had been liberated, and UNITA was disintegrating into such disorder that an MPLA rocket in Gago Cutinho destroyed the house Jonas Savimbi had occupied only an hour before.

In mid-March, South African troops began to retreat. The order must have come from the top, for fear that the MPLA's pursuit would continue into occupied Namibia and carry the war right up to South African territory. Such an action would undoubtedly have had the support of all black Africa and of the great majority of the countries in the United Nations that opposed racial discrimination. Cuban combatants had no doubt this was the aim when they were ordered en masse to the Southern Front. But on April 1, when the fleeing South Africans crossed the border and took refuge in Namibia, the only order the MPLA received was to occupy the abandoned dams and guarantee the safety of the workers of all nationalities.

On April 1, at 9:15 a.m., the MPLA advance forces under Cuban commander Leopoldo Cintra Frías reached the Ruacaná dam, at the very edge of the chicken-wire fence that marks the border. An hour and a quarter later, the South African governor of Namibia, General Ewefp,[5] accompanied by two other officers, asked for authorization to cross the border and begin conversations with the MPLA. Commander Cintra Frías received them in a wooden shed built on a neutral stretch of ground ten meters wide separating the two countries. The delegates from both sides and their interpreters sat down to talk at a long dining-room table. General Ewefp—a man of fifty or so, heavy and balding, someone who did his best to convey the image of an amiable individual with a lot of experience in

---

5. At the meeting, which actually occurred March 27, 1976, Pretoria's delegation was headed by Johannes Marthinius de Wet, commissioner general of the South African colony of Namibia.

GABRIEL GARCÍA MÁRQUEZ

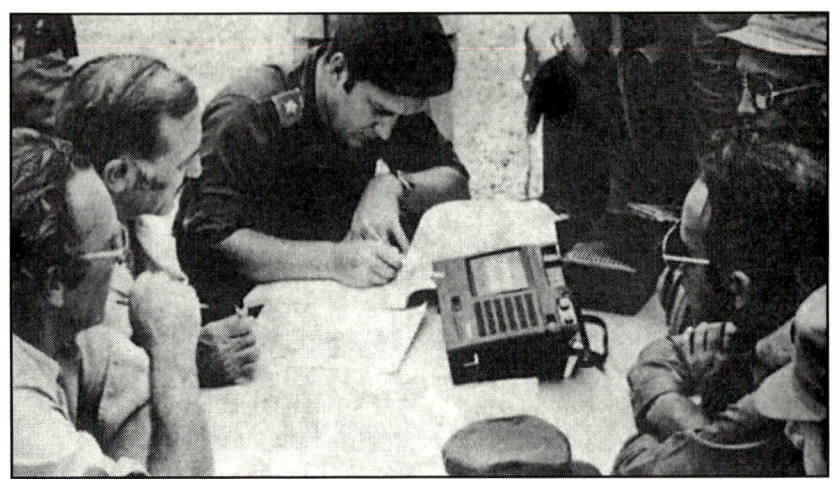

After Pretoria's forces were driven out of Angola at the end of March 1976, South African officials governing Namibia asked permission to cross border and initiate talks. In agreement signed March 27, they turned over to Angola control of the Ruacaná and Calueque dams under construction at the Namibia-Angola frontier.
Left: March 27, 1976. From left, J. Thompson, general construction manager; J.M. de Wet, South African government representative in Namibia (still called South-West Africa by Pretoria); and South African army representative. To right (in cap and sunglasses), Leopoldo Cintra Frías, commander of Cuban forces in Angola and head of Cuban-Angolan delegation. **Right:** Cuban tank commander Nestor López Cuba (third from left, facing camera and wearing hat) and Cuban officer Jorge Guerrero (right) during discussions that same day at border. Men with backs to camera are South Africans.

the world—unconditionally accepted the MPLA's terms. Two hours were spent on the agreement but the meeting took much longer since General Ewefp ordered a sumptuous lunch brought in from the Namibian side. While everyone was eating, he made toasts with beer and told his adversaries how he had lost the little finger of his right hand in an auto accident.

At the end of May, Henry Kissinger visited Prime Minister Olof Palme in Stockholm and, upon emerging from the meeting, jubilantly declared to the world press that Cuban troops were being withdrawn from Angola. The news came, it was said, in a personal letter Fidel Castro had sent Palme. Kissinger's joy was understandable because the withdrawal of Cuban troops lifted a burden off his back in dealing with US public opinion, agitated by the election campaign.

The truth is that Fidel Castro had sent no letter to Palme on this occasion. Palme's information, however, was correct but incomplete. In reality, the timetable for withdrawing Cuban troops from Angola had been agreed to by Fidel Castro and Agostinho Neto when they met in Conakry, Guinea, on March 14, when victory was already a fact. They decided the withdrawal would be gradual. As many Cuban troops as necessary would remain in Angola as long as necessary to organize a strong, modern army capable of guaranteeing the country's internal security and independence in the future, without aid from anyone.

So when Henry Kissinger committed that indiscretion in Stockholm, more than three thousand Cuban troops had already returned from Angola and many others were on their way back. Here, too, an effort was made to keep their return secret for security reasons. But Esther Lilia Díaz Rodríguez, the first woman who went to Angola and one of the first who returned by plane, offered proof once again of the ingenuity of Cubans in finding out everything. Esther had been sent to the Havana Naval Hospital for the required medical checkup before her family was notified of her return. After forty-eight hours she was authorized to leave the hospital and she took a taxi on the corner. The driver took her to her home without comment. He refused, however, to take the fare because he knew she had just returned from Angola. "How did you know?" Esther asked him, perplexed. The driver answered, "Because I saw you yesterday on the hospital terrace, and that terrace is reserved for those returning from Angola."

134   OPERATION CARLOTA

I arrived in Havana during those days, and even at the airport I had the definite impression that something very profound had happened in Cuban life since I had last been there a year before. The change was indefinable but quite evident—not only in people's mood but also in the very nature of things—animals, sea, in the very character of Cuban life. There was a new men's fashion for lightweight suits with short-sleeved jackets. Portuguese words had found their way into the language heard in the streets. There were new strains in the old African rhythms of popular music. Discussions were noisier than usual in the lines in front of stores and in the crowded buses, between those who had been determined partisans of the action in Angola and those just now beginning to grasp what it meant.

The most interesting—and striking—experience, however, was the awareness of many returning combatants that they had contributed to changing the history of the world, even though they conducted themselves with the naturalness and modesty of those who had simply done their duty.

Perhaps they themselves did not realize that on another level—which while less noble might also be more human—even Cubans lacking in great passion felt compensated for the many years of unfair setbacks they had had to live through. In 1970, when the ten-million-ton sugar harvest failed, Fidel Castro asked the people to turn defeat into victory. In reality, Cubans had been doing that for too long, with a tenacious political consciousness and an unassailable moral strength.

Since the victory at the Bay of Pigs more than fifteen years earlier, Cubans had to accept, with gritted teeth, the murder of Che Guevara in Bolivia and of President Salvador Allende during the Chile catastrophe; they had witnessed the extermination of the guerrillas in Latin America, the endless night of blockade, and the hidden, implacable gnawing of those many past domestic mistakes that at times brought them to the brink of disaster. All these experiences, separate from the irreversible but slow and hard-won victories of the revolution, must have created in Cubans the feeling they were being subjected to an undeserved penance. Angola, finally, gave them the satisfaction of the great victory they so much needed.

GLOSSARY OF INDIVIDUALS, ORGANIZATIONS, AND EVENTS

Acevedo, Enrique (1942–) – Brigadier general; writer and historian of Cuba's armed forces. Served in Angola 1977 and 1987–88, commanding tank brigade. Joined Rebel Army July 1957 at age 14. Later assigned to Che Guevara's Column 8 that crossed Cuba from Sierra Maestra mountains to the Escambray.

Agramonte, Ignacio (1841–1873) – One of principal political and military leaders of Cuba's first independence war against Spain. Division commander of Liberation Army in Camagüey province, rose to rank of major general. Killed in battle.

Baraguá Protest – *See* Maceo, Antonio

Batista, Fulgencio (1901–1973) – Military strongman in Cuba 1934–58. Elected president 1940–44. Led March 1952 coup establishing US-backed military-police tyranny. Fled Cuba January 1, 1959, in face of advancing Rebel Army and popular insurrection.

Bay of Pigs – *See* Playa Girón

Cabral, Amilcar (1924–1973) – Founding leader of African Party for the Independence of Guinea and Cape Verde (PAIGC) 1956. In 1963 PAIGC took up arms against Portuguese rule, winning Guinea-Bissau's independence in 1974 and Cape Verde's in 1975. Assassinated January 1973.

Carlota – A slave from the Triunvirato sugar mill in Matanzas, Cuba, who led a rebellion that began Nov. 5, 1843. She was captured and killed as the rebellion was crushed.

Cassinga – Namibian refugee camp in southern Angola, attacked in May 1978 by South African jets armed with thousand-pound bombs followed by paratroopers. More than 600 residents were massacred, nearly half of them children. Hundreds of surviving children, many wounded, were brought to Cuba, where they received medical care and schooling.

Castro, Fidel (1926–) – Central leader of revolutionary movement in Cuba since beginning of struggle against Batista dictatorship in 1952. Organized July 26, 1953, attack on Moncada garrison in Santiago de Cuba and Carlos Manuel de Céspedes garrison in Bayamo. Captured and sentenced to 15 years in prison. Released 1955 after amnesty campaign. Led fusion of revolutionary organizations to found July 26 Revolutionary Movement. Organized *Granma* expedition from Mexico to launch revolutionary war in Cuba 1956. Commander in chief Rebel Army 1956–59 and commander in chief Revolutionary Armed Forces 1959–2008. Cuba's prime minister, February 1959 to 1976. First secretary Communist Party of Cuba 1965–2011; president of Council of State and Council of Ministers 1976–2008.

Castro, Raúl (1931–) – President of Council of State and Council of Ministers since 2008 and first secretary of Communist Party of Cuba since 2011. An organizer of student protests at University of Havana against Batista dictatorship, he participated in 1953 Moncada attack and was captured and sentenced to 13 years in prison. Released May 1955 following amnesty campaign. Founding member of July 26 Movement and participant in *Granma* expedition. Rebel Army commander of Second Eastern Front 1958. Minister of Revolutionary Armed Forces 1959–2008. Vice premier 1959–76. First vice president of Council of State and Council of Ministers 1976–2008 and second secretary of Communist Party 1965–2011.

Céspedes, Carlos Manuel de (1819–1874) – A plantation owner, he freed his slaves in October 1868 and launched first war against Spanish colonial rule. Supreme commander of Cuban independence army; killed in battle February 27, 1874.

Choy, Armando (1934–) – Brigadier general; president State Working Group for the Cleanup, Preservation, and Development of Havana Bay. Deputy head of Antiaircraft Defense and Air Force in Angola 1980–81. Ambassador to Cape Verde 1986–92. Member July 26 Movement since 1955; joined its guerrilla unit in Escambray mountains May 1958, later promoted to Rebel Army captain. Commanded one of infantry battalions at Playa Girón, April 1961. Founding member Communist Party of Cuba.

Chui, Gustavo (1938–) – Brigadier general. Helped establish internationalist military missions in Mozambique, Ethiopia, Nicaragua. Head of staff in 1975 of command post in Cuba assisting Fidel Castro and Raúl Castro in directing Angola mission. Deputy chief of staff in Angola 1986–87; headed 90th Tank Brigade in Malanje province 1987–88. Gravely wounded by antitank mine. Joined Rebel Army early 1958. Organized arming of militia and army units that fought mercenaries at Playa Girón, April 1961. Founding member Communist Party of Cuba.

Cintra Frías, Leopoldo (Polo, Polito) (1941–) – Army corps general and since 2011 minister of Revolutionary Armed Forces and member of Council of State. Member of Communist Party Central Committee since founding in 1965 and of its Political Bureau since 1991. Served in internationalist mission in Ethiopia in 1978 as head of tank brigade; commanded forces on Angola's Southern Front 1975–76. Headed Cuba's military mission in Angola 1983–86 and 1989. A Hero of the Republic of Cuba. From peasant family near Yara in eastern Cuba, joined Rebel Army November 1957. Finished revolutionary war as a lieutenant, promoted to captain January 1959.

Colomé, Abelardo (Furry) (1939–) – Army corps general and, since 1989, minister of interior. Member of Communist Party Central Committee since founding in 1965. Member of Political Bureau of Communist Party and Council of State. Head of Cuban mission in Angola 1975–76. Hero of Republic of Cuba. Joined July 26 Movement 1955. Participant in Nov. 30, 1956, armed action in Santiago de Cuba. Part of first reinforcements sent to Rebel Army in Sierra Maestra March 1957. Promoted to commander December 1958. Internationalist mission in Argentina and Bolivia 1962–64 to prepare guerrilla front in Argentina led by Jorge Ricardo Masetti.

Cuban Five – Gerardo Hernández, Ramón Labañino, Antonio Guerrero, Fernando González, and René González. Five Cubans who in 1990s accepted internationalist missions to monitor plans of Cuban American counterrevolutionary groups in southern Florida engaged in violent attacks on Cuban Revolution. Arrested by FBI in September 1998 and framed up on more than 30 charges, from acting as unregistered agents of the Cuban government to conspiracy to commit espionage and murder. Convicted and given sentences ranging from 15 years for René González to double life for Gerardo Hernández, who led the group. As of 2013 had spent more than 14 years in captivity. Campaign fighting for their release has grown worldwide.

Cuban independence wars – From 1868 to 1898 Cubans waged three wars for independence from Spain: Ten Years War (1868–78), "Little War" (1879–80), and war of 1895–98, which ended Spanish rule. The US government occupied the island after Spain's defeat and imposed so-called Platt Amendment on Cuba's constitution, authorizing Washington to "exercise the right to intervene" in Cuba and to establish naval bases on the island.

De la Guardia Font, Antonio (Tony) (1938–1989) – Colonel in Ministry of Interior, where he headed special forces for 18 years. In 1987 became head of Interior Ministry department organized to circumvent US economic embargo. Used position in that agency to engage in drug-trafficking operations. In June–July 1989 arrested, tried, convicted, and executed along with Division General Arnaldo Ochoa and two other high-ranking officers of Revolutionary Armed Forces and Interior Ministry.

De la Torriente Brau, Pablo (1901–1936) – Journalist and fighter in early 1930s against Gerardo Machado dictatorship. A volunteer for the republic in Spain's civil war, he was killed in battle December 1936.

Díaz Argüelles, Raúl (1936–1975) – First head of Cuba's internationalist mission in Angola; killed by land mine December 1975 and posthumously promoted to brigadier general. In early 1970s headed Revolutionary Armed Forces 10th Directorate, which oversaw assistance to anti-imperialist movements in Latin America and Africa and Cuba's internationalist missions. A member of Revolutionary Directorate in Havana during anti-Batista struggle, he joined its guerrilla column in Escambray mountains 1958. Became Rebel Army commander.

Dos Santos, Jose Eduardo (1942–) – President of Angola since 1979, following death of founding leader Agostinho Neto. Joined MPLA 1956. Minister of foreign affairs after independence 1976.

Espinosa Martín, Ramón (1939–) – Army corps general and since 2009 vice minister Revolutionary Armed Forces. Served in Angola 1975–76 as head of Cuban forces in Cabinda, seriously wounded by antitank mine. Member of Communist Party Central Committee since 1980; Political Bureau since 1997. Head of Cuban military mission in Ethiopia 1980–82. Head of Eastern Army 1982–2010. Hero of the Republic of Cuba. Member of July 26 Movement late 1956. Joined Revolutionary Directorate guerrilla column in Escambray 1958, finishing war as first lieutenant.

FAPLA (People's Armed Forces for the Liberation of Angola) – Originating as armed wing of MPLA in fight against Portuguese colonialism, became Angola's armed forces following independence in 1975.

FLEC (Front for the Liberation of the Enclave of Cabinda) – Formed 1963 to fight Portuguese colonial rule in Cabinda. Following Angola's independence in 1975, FLEC forces fought MPLA-led Angolan government, advocating separation for oil-rich Cabinda. Received backing from UNITA, regime in Zaire, and Washington.

FNLA (National Front for the Liberation of Angola) – Formed 1962 and led by Holden Roberto. One of armed groups in struggle against Portuguese colonialism; developed ties with CIA and dictatorship in Zaire. Backed by Zaire and South Africa, waged war against Angolan government following independence in 1975.

Girón – *See* Playa Girón

Gómez, Máximo (1836–1905) – Born in Dominican Republic, he fought in pro-independence war in Cuba 1868–78. Major general of Liberation Army by end of conflict. When war relaunched in 1895, returned to Cuba as general in chief of Cuban independence army.

González Llort, Fernando (1963–) – One of five Cuban revolutionaries imprisoned in US since 1998 (see glossary, Cuban Five). Went to Florida 1997; carried out mission monitoring violent counterrevolutionary groups until arrest by FBI in September 1998. Framed and convicted on two counts of acting and causing others to act as unregistered agent of a foreign government; conspiracy to do so; and two other counts. Sentenced to 19 years, later reduced to 17 years and 9 months. Served in Cuba's internationalist mission in Angola in intelligence unit in Southern Front 1987–89. Member Communist Party of Cuba since 1988. Hero of the Republic of Cuba.

González Sehwerert, René (1956–) – One of five Cuban revolutionaries held in US prisons since 1998 (see glossary, Cuban Five). Flew "stolen" plane from Cuba to US in 1990. Joined counterrevolutionary group Brothers to the Rescue and other paramilitary outfits and reported to Cuban government on planned actions. Carried out mission until arrest by FBI in September 1998. Convicted of acting as unregistered agent of a foreign government and conspiracy to do so; served over 13 years of a 15-year sentence. Paroled October 2011 on court-supervised release in US until 2014. Served in Cuba's internationalist mission in Angola 1977–79. Member Communist Party of Cuba since 1990. Hero of the Republic of Cuba.

Granma – On Dec. 2, 1956, eighty-two revolutionary combatants led by Fidel Castro landed in southeast Cuba on the boat *Granma*, following seven-day journey from Mexico. Despite initial setbacks, guerrilla fighters established base for Rebel Army in Sierra Maestra mountains. From there they led workers and peasants in revolutionary war against Batista dictatorship; extended clandestine July 26 Movement across Cuba; and deepened social revolution in liberated territories, establishing embryo of new state.

Guerrero Rodríguez, Antonio (1958–) – One of five Cuban revolutionaries imprisoned in US since 1998 (see glossary, Cuban Five). Went to Florida 1992; carried out mission monitoring counterrevolutionary groups there until arrest by FBI in September 1998. Framed and convicted of conspiracy to commit espionage and two other charges. Given life sentence, later reduced to 21 years and 10 months. Graduated with civil engineering degree from University of Kiev in Ukraine. Has published book of poetry written behind bars, and paintings done in prison have been exhibited internationally. Member Communist Party of Cuba since 1989. Hero of the Republic of Cuba.

Guevara, Ernesto Che (1928–1967) – Born in Argentina, Guevara became one of central leaders of the Cuban Revolution. Joined *Granma* expedition in Mexico as troops' doctor. Became guerrilla commander in Rebel Army and held leading responsibilities in new revolutionary government, including head of National Bank and minister of industry. In early 1965 visited Africa and met with leaders of liberation organizations fighting Portuguese colonial rule. Later that year resigned government posts and left Cuba to prepare participation in revolutionary struggles in Southern Cone of Latin America. Led volunteer mission in eastern Congo in 1965 to aid anti-imperialist forces. Went to Bolivia 1966 to lead guerrilla movement against military dictatorship there. Captured and killed October 1967 by Bolivian army in CIA-directed operation.

Guiteras, Antonio (1906–1935) – Leader of anti-imperialist forces during 1933 revolution that toppled Gerardo Machado dictatorship. Interior minister in "Hundred Days Government" overthrown in January 1934 "Sergeants' Revolt" led by Batista. Murdered in January 1935 while leading revolutionary struggle against military regime.

Hernández Nordelo, Gerardo (1965–) – One of five Cuban revolutionaries imprisoned in US since 1998 (see glossary, Cuban Five). Came to Florida in 1994; headed internationalist mission to monitor plans of counterrevolutionary groups engaged in violent actions against Cuban Revolution. Arrested by FBI in September 1998. Framed and convicted on charges of conspiracy to gather and transmit national defense information to a foreign government, conspiracy to murder, and 11 other counts. Given two life sentences. An accomplished cartoonist, his prison drawings have been exhibited around the world. Commanded reconnaissance platoon in Cabinda during 1989–90 internationalist mission in Angola. Member Communist Party of Cuba since 1993. Hero of the Republic of Cuba.

Kabila, Laurent (1939–2001) – Opposed 1960 Belgian- and US-backed coup that brought down newly independent government in Congo headed by Patrice Lumumba. Helped lead 1964 rebellion against proimperialist regime of Joseph Kasavubu and Moise Tshombe. A leader of Congolese forces assisted in 1965 by Cuban internationalist column headed by Guevara. Following ouster of Mobutu dictatorship in 1997, Kabila became country's head of state. Assassinated January 2001.

Labañino Salazar, Ramón (1963–) – One of five Cuban revolutionaries imprisoned in US since 1998 (see glossary, Cuban Five). Went to Florida 1992; second in command of mission monitoring counterrevolutionary groups engaged in violent attacks on Cuban Revolution. Arrested by FBI September 1998. Framed and convicted of conspiracy to gather and transmit national defense information to a foreign government and on 9 other counts. Sentenced to life in prison, later reduced to 30 years. Joined Union of Young Communists 1987. Officer of Ministry of the Interior since 1988. Member Communist Party of Cuba since 1991. Hero of the Republic of Cuba.

López Cuba, Nestor (1938–1999) – At his death a division general of Revolutionary Armed Forces, member of Central Committee of Communist Party, and vice president of the executive secretariat of Association of Combatants of the Cuban Revolution. Served on internationalist missions in Syria 1973, Angola 1975–76 as head of tank column on Southern Front. After 1979 headed Cuba's military mission to Nicaragua during war against US-backed counterrevolutionary forces. Joined July 26 Movement 1957 and Rebel Army May 1958.

Lumumba, Patrice (1925–1961) – Leader of independence struggle in Congo and prime minister after independence from Belgium in June 1960. In

September, after requesting United Nations troops to block attacks by imperialist-backed mercenaries, his government was overthrown in coup instigated by Belgium and the US. UN troops supposedly guarding Lumumba facilitated his capture and murder by proimperialist forces in January 1961.

Maceo, Antonio (1845–1896) – Military leader in Cuba's 19th century wars of independence from Spain. Known in Cuba as the Bronze Titan. At conclusion of first war in 1878, became symbol of revolutionary intransigence by refusing to put down arms in action known as Baraguá Protest. Killed in battle.

Mandela, Nelson (1918–) – Leader of anti-apartheid struggle and African National Congress of South Africa from mid-1940s. Arrested in 1962 and imprisoned until 1990. Released amid advancing mass revolutionary struggle to bring down white supremacist regime, which was given major boost by apartheid army's 1988 defeat in Angola. Elected president of South Africa in first post-apartheid election in 1994, serving until 1999.

Martí, José (1853–1895) – Cuba's national hero, Martí was a noted poet and writer. Arrested and exiled for independence activity at age 16. Founded Cuban Revolutionary Party in 1892. Led fight to oppose Spanish colonial rule and US designs on Cuba. Organized and planned 1895 independence war; killed in battle.

Mambises – Fighters in Cuba's three wars of independence from Spain between 1868 and 1898. Many were former slaves and Chinese bonded laborers. The term "mambí" is of African origin.

Mella, Julio Antonio (1903–1929) – A founding leader of Communist Party of Cuba 1925. Arrested 1926, escaped to Mexico, continuing to organize against Gerardo Machado dictatorship. Assassinated in Mexico City by Machado agent January 1929.

Mobutu Sese Seko (1930–1997) – Army chief of staff in newly independent Congo; led 1960 proimperialist coup against Patrice Lumumba. In 1965 proclaimed himself president, holding power until overthrown in 1997. Born Joseph Mobutu, he changed his name in 1972.

Moncada attack – On July 26, 1953, some 160 combatants under command of Fidel Castro launched simultaneous insurrectionary attacks on Moncada army garrison in Santiago de Cuba and a garrison in Bayamo, opening revolutionary struggle against Batista dictatorship. Five killed in combat at Moncada. After attack's failure, Batista's forces massacred 56 captured revolutionaries. Fidel Castro and others were arrested six days later; he and 31 others were sentenced to up to 15 years in prison. Broad national amnesty campaign won their release May 15, 1955.

Moracén Limonta, Rafael (1939–) – Brigadier general; from 2008 military attaché to Cuban embassy in Angola. Served on internationalist missions in Congo-Brazzaville 1965–67, Syria 1973, Angola 1975–82. Cuban advisor to commander of Angolan president Agostinho Neto's presidential guard. Joined Rebel Army's Third Eastern Front commanded by Juan Almeida 1958. Hero of the Republic of Cuba.

MPLA (Popular Movement for the Liberation of Angola) – Founded 1956 to wage armed struggle for Angola's independence from Portugal. From 1962 led by Agostinho Neto. Following independence in 1975 became governing party.

Neto, Agostinho (1922–1979) – Leader of fight against Portuguese colonialism in Angola. Elected president of MPLA at its first national conference in 1962; jailed and exiled several times for anticolonial activity. Met with Ernesto Che Guevara during his 1965 tour of African countries and requested Cuba's aid for independence struggle. President of Angola 1975 until his death. Elected MPLA's general secretary at its first postindependence congress in 1977.

Ochoa, Arnaldo (1940–1989) – Former division general, member of Communist Party Central Committee 1965–89. Participated in internationalist mission in Venezuela 1960s; headed Cuban military missions in Ethiopia 1970s, Nicaragua 1983–86, Angola 1987–88. Claiming desire to raise funds for military materials, while heading mission in Angola he supervised black market operations; directed smuggling of ivory, diamonds, and other contraband; and organized subordinates to work with Medellín drug cartel and other traffickers, using Cuban air and sea lanes. In June–July 1989 he and three other high-ranking officers of Revolutionary

Armed Forces and Ministry of the Interior were arrested, tried, convicted, and executed for these and related acts. At same trial, 13 other Cuban army and Ministry of Interior officers were convicted and given prison sentences of up to 30 years.

October 1962 "Missile" Crisis – In face of Washington's preparations to invade, Cuban government signed mutual defense agreement with Soviet Union in 1962. In October 1962 US president John Kennedy demanded removal of Soviet nuclear missiles from Cuba, ordered naval blockade, stepped up invasion plans, and placed US armed forces on nuclear alert. Cuban workers and farmers mobilized in millions to defend revolution. On Oct. 28 Soviet premier Nikita Khrushchev, without consulting Cuban government, announced decision to remove missiles.

Paris Communards – Participants in first attempt in history by working people to establish their own revolutionary government, the Paris Commune. Workers, artisans, and other toilers held power from March 18 to May 28, 1871, when their resistance was crushed by the forces of the French bourgeoisie. In the ensuing terror more than 20,000 working people of Paris were massacred.

Playa Girón – On April 17, 1961, 1,500 Cuban mercenaries organized, financed, and deployed by Washington invaded Cuba at Bay of Pigs on southern coast. In fewer than 72 hours of combat, mercenaries were defeated by Cuba's revolutionary militias, armed forces, and police. On April 19 remaining invaders were captured at Playa Girón (Girón Beach), the name used in Cuba for those days of combat.

Portuguese revolution – In April 1974 Portugal's dictatorship, in power since late 1920s, was toppled in coup by military officers, unleashing revolutionary working-class upsurge. Key factor in regime's fall was growing strength of liberation struggles against Portuguese colonial rule in Africa. Revolutionary upheaval in Portugal was undermined by Communist and Socialist party leaderships, which collaborated with capitalist rulers to consolidate new bourgeois regime by early 1976.

Rectification process – Political course implemented by Cuban revolutionary leadership between 1986 and 1991. Marked turn away from copying anti-working-class, bureaucratic political and economic policies long entrenched in Soviet Union and Eastern Europe. An aspect of earlier political retreat was dwindling use of voluntary labor, which had been promoted by Cuban leadership during revolution's opening years as a proletarian lever enabling working people to bring weight to bear through shared social labor. During rectification voluntary work was revived as popular mass course to address pressing social needs such as child care centers, schools, clinics, housing, and to counter growth of privileged bureaucratic layers. Deep economic crisis of Special Period from early 1990s brought end to large-scale volunteer work brigades and contingents.

Resolution 435 – *See* UN Security Council Resolution 435.

Revolutionary Armed Forces (FAR) – Continuator of Rebel Army, led by Fidel Castro, that waged Cuba's 1956–58 revolutionary war. FAR was established October 1959, consolidating under single command structure Rebel Army, Rebel Air Force, Revolutionary Navy, and Revolutionary National Police. Raúl Castro became head of Ministry of the Revolutionary Armed Forces (MINFAR) at its inception, a responsibility he held until 2008.

Risquet Valdés Saldaña, Jorge (1930–) – Headed civilian mission in Angola 1975–79. In late 1965 and 1966 commanded Column 2 of Cuban internationalist combatants sent to Congo-Brazzaville to support Column 1 led by Che Guevara assisting liberation forces in eastern region of former Belgian Congo. While there organized Cuban collaboration with and aid for MPLA.

Roberto, Holden (1923–2007) – Cofounded Angola's first independence movement 1956. In 1962 founding leader of FNLA. Worked with CIA and proimperialist Mobutu dictatorship in Zaire.

Rodiles Planas, Samuel (1932–) – Division general, president of National Association of Combatants of the Cuban Revolution. Chief of staff of office of minister of Revolutionary Armed Forces. Since 2012 president Cuba's National Assembly Defense Commission and of national institute for urban land use planning. Served in Angola 1977, 1978, and as commander of mission 1989–91. Last Cuban soldier to board final plane leaving Angola. Hero of the Republic of Cuba. Joined July 26 Movement in Guantánamo in 1955, combatant in Second Eastern Front from March 1958, promoted to commander December 1958.

Savimbi, Jonas (1934–2002) – In 1960 joined movement for Angola's independence from Portugal. Founded UNITA in 1966; its central leader. In 1975 allied with South Africa and US to overthrow new MPLA-led government. Led civil war against government for more than 25 years. Killed in battle with Angolan government forces.

Schueg Colás, Víctor (1936–1998) – Brigadier general in FAR. Head of Central Army 1987–88. Alternate member Communist Party Central Committee 1980–86, full member 1986–91. Carried out internationalist mission in Congo in 1965 as part of Che Guevara's column. Served in Angola 1975–76 as chief of staff of Cuban military mission. Joined Rebel Army 1958, serving under Raúl Castro.

Sékou Touré, Ahmed (1922–1984) – Leader of struggle for independence from France in what is today Republic of Guinea, whose capital is Conakry. Became president of country at independence in 1958, serving until his death.

Sío Wong, Moisés (1938–2010) – Brigadier general. At his death, president of National Institute of State Reserves since 1986, and president Cuba-China Friendship Association. Served in Angola as head of logistics 1976. Joined Rebel Army 1957, serving in Column 1 commanded by Fidel Castro and Column 8 led by Ernesto Che Guevara. During 1961 Bay of Pigs invasion headed 7th Infantry Division in Pinar del Río under Guevara's command. Founding member of Communist Party of Cuba. Adjutant to minister of Revolutionary Armed Forces Raúl Castro 1965–72. Headed Cadres Directorate of Revolutionary Armed Forces 1982–85 with responsibility for assigning officers.

Special Period – Term used in Cuba for extremely difficult economic conditions faced during 1990s and policies implemented to defend revolution. With fall of Stalinist regimes in Eastern Europe and USSR, Cuba lost 85 percent of its foreign trade. Consequences were compounded by accelerating world capitalist crisis and intensified economic warfare by Washington. Facing deepest economic crisis since 1959, revolutionary government in 1993–94 adopted measures to address worsening conditions. By 1996, through efforts by Cuban working people, a recovery began. Agricultural and industrial production remained far below pre-1990 levels, however, resulting in severe shortages of food and other essentials.

SWAPO (South West Africa People's Organisation) – National liberation movement formed 1960 to fight for Namibia's independence from South African rule. Fought alongside Cuban-Angolan forces in southern Angola. Party has headed Namibian government since independence in 1990.

UN Security Council Resolution 435 – Adopted in 1978. Called for South Africa to surrender control of South-West Africa (Namibia) and outlined steps for UN-supervised elections to establish independent government.

UNITA (National Union for the Total Independence of Angola) – Founded 1964 to fight Portuguese colonial rule, led by Jonas Savimbi. In 1975 allied with apartheid South Africa and Washington in effort to overthrow MPLA-led government of newly independent country. Over next 25 years waged war against Angolan government. UNITA signed cease-fire in March 2002, a month after Savimbi was killed in battle with government forces.

Valdés, Ramiro (1932–) – Member of Communist Party Central Committee since 1965; Political Bureau 1965–86 and again since 2008. Vice president of Council of State and Council of Ministers since 2010. Minister of Interior 1961–68, 1979–85. One of the three Sierra combatants to hold title Commander of the Revolution. A truck driver and carpenter, he participated in 1953 Moncada attack. Sentenced to ten years in prison and released May 1955 following amnesty campaign. *Granma* expeditionary. Commander of Rebel Army Column 4 in Sierra Maestra and second in command of Column 8 under Che Guevara in march to Las Villas.

Van Heerden, Neil (1939–) – Director general of apartheid South Africa's Ministry of Foreign Affairs in 1980s. Involved in negotiations with Cuba and Angola over end of war.

Zayas, Luis Alfonso (1936–) – Brigadier general; director of administration of Association of Combatants of the Cuban Revolution. Served three missions in Angola 1975–76, 1977–78, and 1985–87. Joined July 26 Movement in 1956; carried out sabotage action in preparation for *Granma* landing. Member of first group of reinforcements to Rebel Army, March 1957, fought under Ernesto Che Guevara's command in Column 8. In 1959 in charge of La Cabaña prison, where dictatorship's murderers were tried by revolutionary tribunals. Member of Central Committee of Communist Party 1965–86. Second in command Youth Army of Labor, units of Armed Forces engaged primarily in agricultural labor 1987–98.

"One of the ways our revolution will be judged in years to come is by how well we have solved the problems facing women."

FIDEL CASTRO, 1974

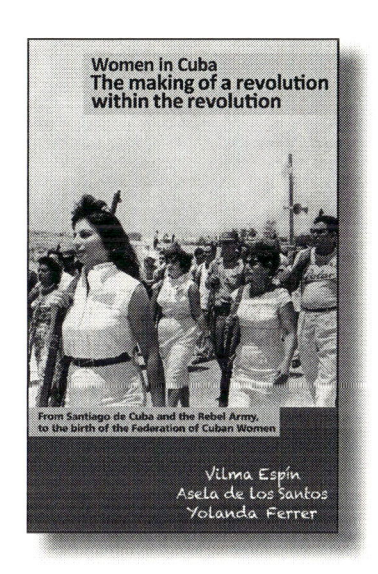

As working people in Cuba fought to bring down a bloody tyranny in the 1950s, the unprecedented integration of women in the ranks and leadership of the struggle was not an aberration. It was inseparably intertwined with the proletarian course of the leadership of the Cuban Revolution from the start.

Women in Cuba: The Making of a Revolution Within the Revolution is the story of that revolution and how it transformed the women and men who made it.

The book was introduced at the 2012 Havana International Book Fair by a panel of speakers from Cuba and the US.

Women and Revolution: The Living Example of the Cuban Revolution contains the presentations from that event. The example set by the men and women who made the Cuban Revolution, says Mary-Alice Waters, "is an indispensable armament in the tumultuous class battles whose initial skirmishes are already upon us."

Women in Cuba: The Making of a Revolution Within the Revolution

Vilma Espín
Asela de los Santos
Yolanda Ferrer
$20

&

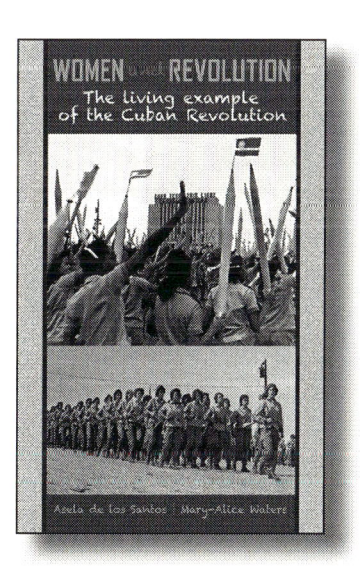

Women and Revolution: The Living Example of the Cuban Revolution

Asela de los Santos
Mary-Alice Waters
$7

Both titles also in Spanish.

WWW.PATHFINDERPRESS.COM

THE FIGHT FOR WOMEN'S EMANCIPATION

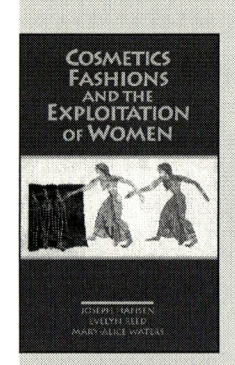

Cosmetics, Fashions, and the Exploitation of Women
Joseph Hansen, Evelyn Reed
Introduction by Mary-Alice Waters
How big business uses women's second-class status and social insecurities to market cosmetics and rake in profits. The introduction by Waters explains how the entry of millions of women into the workforce during and after World War II irreversibly changed US society and laid the basis for a renewed rise of struggles for women's emancipation. $15

Problems of Women's Liberation
Evelyn Reed
Explores the social and economic roots of women's oppression from prehistoric society to modern capitalism and points the road forward to emancipation. $15

The Origin of the Family, Private Property, and the State
Frederick Engels
Introduction by Evelyn Reed
How the emergence of class-divided society gave rise to repressive state bodies and family structures that protect the property of the ruling layers and enable them to preserve wealth and privilege. Engels discusses the consequences for working people, male and female, of these class institutions—from their original forms to their modern versions. $18

Abortion Is a Woman's Right!
Pat Grogan, Evelyn Reed
Why abortion rights are central not only to the fight for the full emancipation of women, but to forging a united and fighting labor movement. $6. Also in Spanish.

New International
A MAGAZINE OF MARXIST POLITICS AND THEORY

NO. 13
Our Politics Start with the World by Jack Barnes, Steve Clark • **Farming, Science, and the Working Classes** by Steve Clark • **Capitalism, Labor, and Nature: An Exchange** by Richard Levins, Steve Clark $14

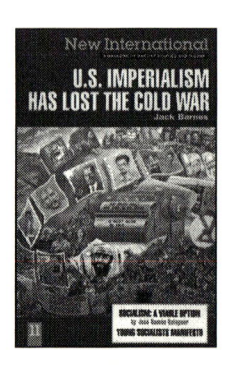

NO. 11
U.S. Imperialism Has Lost the Cold War by Jack Barnes • **The Communist Strategy of Party Building Today** by Mary-Alice Waters • **Socialism: A Viable Option** by José Ramón Balaguer • **Young Socialists Manifesto** • **Ours Is the Epoch of World Revolution** by Jack Barnes and Mary-Alice Waters $16

NO. 8
The Politics of Economics: Che Guevara and Marxist Continuity by Steve Clark and Jack Barnes • **Che's Contribution to the Cuban Economy** by Carlos Rafael Rodríguez • **On the Concept of Value** and **The Meaning of Socialist Planning** two articles by Ernesto Che Guevara $10

NO. 6
The Second Assassination of Maurice Bishop by Steve Clark • **Washington's 50-Year Domestic Contra Operation** by Larry Seigle • **Land, Labor, and the Canadian Socialist Revolution** by Michel Dugré • **Renewal or Death: Cuba's Rectification Process** two speeches by Fidel Castro $16

Many of the articles that have appeared in **New International** are also available in Spanish in **Nueva Internacional**, in French in **Nouvelle Internationale**, and in Swedish in **Ny International**.

WWW.PATHFINDERPRESS.COM

From Pathfinder

MALCOLM X, BLACK LIBERATION, AND THE ROAD TO WORKERS POWER
Jack Barnes

"Don't start with Blacks as an oppressed nationality. Start with the vanguard place of workers who are Black in broad proletarian-led struggles in the United States. The record is mind-boggling. It's the strength and resilience, not the oppression, that bowls you over."—Jack Barnes

Drawing lessons from a century and a half of struggle, this book helps us understand why it is the revolutionary conquest of power by the working class that will make possible the final battle for Black freedom—and open the way to a world based not on exploitation, violence, and racism, but human solidarity. A socialist world. $20. Also in Spanish and French.

Companion volume to

THE CHANGING FACE OF U.S. POLITICS
Working-Class Politics and the Trade Unions
Jack Barnes

Building the kind of party working people need to prepare for coming class battles through which they will revolutionize themselves, their unions, and all society. A handbook for those seeking the road toward effective action to overturn the exploitative system of capitalism and join in reconstructing the world on new, socialist foundations. $24. Also in Spanish, French, and Swedish.

THE WORKING CLASS AND THE TRANSFORMATION OF LEARNING
The Fraud of Education Reform under Capitalism
Jack Barnes

"Until society is reorganized so that education is a human activity from the time we are very young until the time we die, there will be no education worthy of working, creating humanity." $3. Also in Spanish, French, Swedish, Icelandic, Farsi, and Greek.

WWW.PATHFINDERPRESS.COM

Cuba's Internationalist

HOW FAR WE SLAVES HAVE COME!
South Africa and Cuba in Today's World
NELSON MANDELA, FIDEL CASTRO

Speaking together in Cuba in 1991, Mandela and Castro discuss the place in the history of Africa of the victory by Cuban, Angolan, and Namibian combatants over the invading US-backed South African army, and the resulting acceleration of the fight to bring down the racist apartheid system. Cuba's internationalist volunteers, said Mandela, made an "unparalleled contribution to African independence, freedom, and justice." $10. Also in Spanish.

IN DEFENSE OF SOCIALISM
Four speeches on the 30th anniversary of the Cuban revolution, 1988–89
FIDEL CASTRO

Castro describes the decisive place of volunteer Cuban fighters in the final stage of the war in Angola against invading forces of South Africa's apartheid regime. Not only is economic and social progress possible without capitalism's dog-eat-dog competition, the Cuban leader says, but socialism is humanity's only way forward. $15

OUR HISTORY IS STILL BEING WRITTEN
The Story of Three Chinese-Cuban Generals in the Cuban Revolution
ARMANDO CHOY, GUSTAVO CHUI, AND MOISÉS SÍO WONG

Three generals of Cuba's Revolutionary Armed Forces talk about the historic place of Chinese immigration to Cuba, as well as over five decades of revolutionary action and internationalism, from Cuba to Angola and Venezuela today. Through their stories we see the social and political forces that gave birth to the Cuban nation and opened the door to socialist revolution in the Americas. $20. Also in Spanish and Chinese.

SOLDIER OF THE CUBAN REVOLUTION
From the Cane Fields of Oriente to General of the Revolutionary Armed Forces
LUIS ALFONSO ZAYAS

The author recounts his experiences over five decades of the revolution. From a teenage combatant in the clandestine struggle and 1956–58 war that brought down the US-backed dictatorship, to serving three times as a leader of the Cuban volunteer forces that helped Angola defeat the army of white-supremacist South Africa, Zayas tells how he and other ordinary men and women in Cuba changed the course of history and, in the process, transformed themselves as well. $18. Also in Spanish.

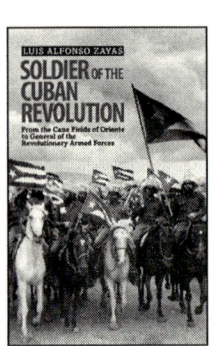

WWW.PATHFINDERPRESS.COM

Mission in Angola

THE CUBAN FIVE
*Who They Are, Why They Were Framed,
Why They Should Be Free*

MARTÍN KOPPEL AND MARY-ALICE WATERS

Five Cuban revolutionists, framed up for being part of a "Cuban spy network" in Florida, have been held in US prisons since 1998. Gerardo Hernández, Ramón Labañino, Antonio Guerrero, Fernando González, and René González—three of whom earlier took part in Cuba's internationalist mission in Angola—were monitoring the plans of rightist groups with a long record of armed attacks on Cuba from US soil. Articles from the *Militant* on the truth about the frame-up and the international fight against it. $5. Third edition. Also in Spanish.

CUBA'S INTERNATIONALIST FOREIGN POLICY
FIDEL CASTRO

Cuba's foreign policy, says Castro, starts "with the subordination of Cuban positions to the international needs of the struggle for socialism and national liberation." Speeches from 1975–80 on solidarity with Angola, Vietnam, the Nicaragua and Grenada revolutions, and more. $23

FROM THE ESCAMBRAY TO THE CONGO
In the Whirlwind of the Cuban Revolution
VÍCTOR DREKE

A leading participant in Cuba's revolutionary movement for more than half a century describes his experiences as second-in-command in the 1965 internationalist mission in Congo led by Che Guevara. Dreke also recounts his participation in the 1956–58 revolutionary war that toppled the US-backed Batista tyranny, as well as his command of volunteer battalions that defeated rightist bands after the revolution's triumph. He describes the creative joy with which working people in Cuba, through such battles at home and abroad, have defended their revolutionary course. $17. Also in Spanish.

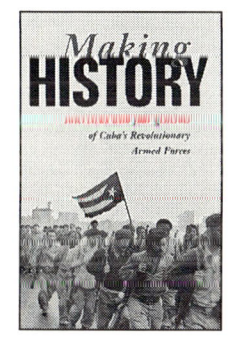

MAKING HISTORY
Interviews with Four Generals of Cuba's Revolutionary Armed Forces
ENRIQUE CARRERAS, NÉSTOR LÓPEZ CUBA,
JOSÉ RAMÓN FERNÁNDEZ, HARRY VILLEGAS

Through the stories of these four outstanding Cuban generals, we can see the class dynamics that have shaped our entire epoch. We can understand how the people of Cuba, as they struggle to build a new society, have for more than fifty years held Washington at bay. Preface by Juan Almeida. $17. Also in Spanish.

Books are part of the 26-title series, "The Cuban Revolution in World Politics," edited and introduced by Mary-Alice Waters.

WWW.PATHFINDERPRESS.COM

PATHFINDER

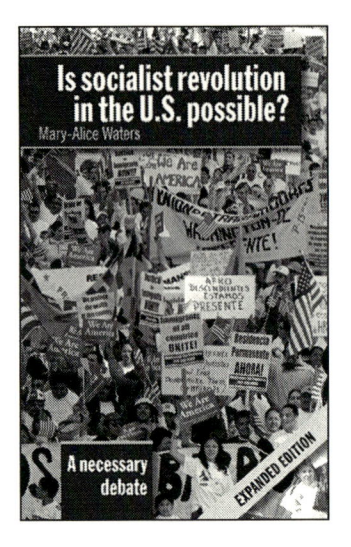

Is Socialist Revolution in the U.S. Possible?
A Necessary Debate
MARY-ALICE WATERS

In two talks—part of a wide-ranging debate at the Venezuela International Book Fairs in 2007 and 2008—Waters explains why a socialist revolution in the US is possible. Why revolutionary struggles by working people are inevitable, forced upon us by the crisis-driven assaults of the propertied classes. As solidarity grows among a fighting vanguard of working people, the outlines of coming class battles can be seen. $7. Also in Spanish, French, and Swedish.

Lenin's Final Fight
Speeches and Writings, 1922–23
V.I. LENIN

In 1922 and 1923, V.I. Lenin, central leader of the world's first socialist revolution, waged what was to be his last political battle. At stake was whether that revolution, and the international movement it led, would remain on the proletarian course that had brought workers and peasants to power in October 1917. Indispensable to understanding how the privileged caste led by Stalin arose and the consequences for the class struggle in the 20th and 21st centuries. $20. Also in Spanish.

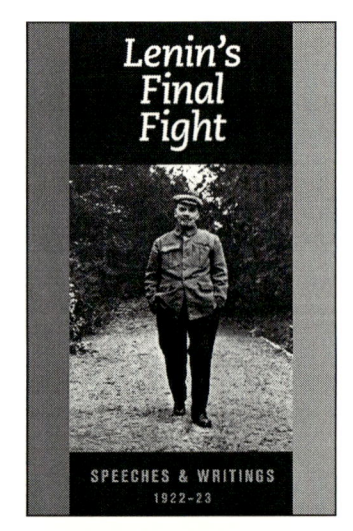

The History of the Russian Revolution
LEON TROTSKY

The social, economic, and political dynamics of the first socialist revolution as told by one of its central leaders. How, under Lenin's leadership, the Bolshevik Party led the overturn of the monarchist regime of the landlords and capitalists and brought to power a government of the workers and peasants. Unabridged, 3 vols. in one. $38. Also in Russian.

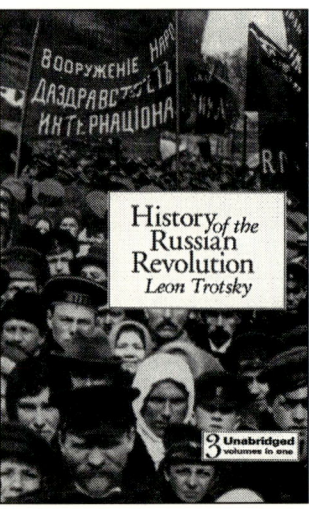

WWW.PATHFINDERPRESS.COM

New International
A MAGAZINE OF MARXIST POLITICS AND THEORY

CAPITALISM'S LONG HOT WINTER HAS BEGUN
Jack Barnes

Today's accelerating global capitalist crisis—the opening stages of what will be decades of economic, financial, and social convulsions and class battles—accompanies a continuation of the most far-reaching shift in Washington's military policy and organization since the US buildup toward World War II. Class-struggle-minded working people must face this historic turning point for imperialism, and draw satisfaction from being "in their face" as we chart a revolutionary course to confront it. In *New International* no. 12. $16. Also in Spanish, French, Swedish, and Arabic.

DEFENDING CUBA, DEFENDING CUBA'S SOCIALIST REVOLUTION
Mary-Alice Waters

In the 1990s, in face of the greatest economic difficulties in the history of the Cuban Revolution, workers and farmers defended their political power, independence and sovereignty, and the historic course they embarked on in 1959. Waters addresses discussions and debates in Cuba on voluntary work, income taxes on wages, farm cooperatives, and much more. In *New International* no. 10. $16. Also in French, Spanish, Farsi, Greek, Icelandic, and Swedish.

Teamster Rebellion
FARRELL DOBBS

The 1934 strikes that built the industrial union movement in Minneapolis and helped pave the way for the CIO, recounted by a central leader of that battle. The first in a four-volume series on the class-struggle leadership of the strikes and organizing drives that transformed the Teamsters union in much of the Midwest into a fighting social movement and pointed the road toward independent labor political action. $19. Also in Spanish, French, and Swedish.

The Jewish Question
A Marxist Interpretation
ABRAM LEON

Traces the historical rationalizations of anti-Semitism to the fact that, in the centuries preceding the domination of industrial capitalism, Jews emerged as a "people-class" of merchants, moneylenders, and traders. Leon explains why the propertied rulers incite renewed Jew-hatred in the epoch of capitalism's decline. $22

Cuba and the Coming American Revolution
JACK BARNES

The Cuban Revolution of 1959 had a worldwide political impact, including on working people and youth in the imperialist heartland. As the mass, proletarian-based struggle for Black rights was already advancing in the US, the social transformation fought for and won by the Cuban toilers set an example that socialist revolution is not only necessary—it can be made and defended. Second edition with a foreword by Mary-Alice Waters. $10. Also in Spanish and French.

February 1965: The Final Speeches
MALCOLM X

Speeches from the last three weeks of the life of this outstanding leader of the working class and the oppressed Black nationality of the United States. A large part was material previously unavailable, with some in print for the first time. $19

WWW.PATHFINDERPRESS.COM

Also from Pathfinder

The Communist Manifesto
KARL MARX, FREDERICK ENGELS

Founding document of the modern revolutionary workers movement, published in 1848. Explains why communism is not a set of preconceived principles but the line of march of the working class toward power, "springing from an existing class struggle, a historical movement going on under our very eyes." $5. Also in Spanish, French, and Arabic.

Socialism: Utopian and Scientific
FREDERICK ENGELS

"To make man the master of his own form of social organization—to make him free—is the historical mission of the modern proletariat," writes Engels. Here socialism is placed on a scientific foundation, the product of the lawful operations of capitalism itself and the struggles of the working class. $12

Revolutionary Continuity
Marxist Leadership in the U.S.
FARRELL DOBBS

How successive generations of fighters joined in the struggles that shaped the US labor movement, seeking to build a class-conscious revolutionary leadership capable of advancing the interests of workers and small farmers and linking up with fellow toilers worldwide. 2 vols. *The Early Years: 1848–1917*, $20; *Birth of the Communist Movement: 1918–1922*, $19.

Thomas Sankara Speaks
The Burkina Faso Revolution, 1983–87

Under Sankara's leadership, the revolutionary government of Burkina Faso in West Africa set an electrifying example. Peasants, workers, women, and youth mobilized to carry out literacy and immunization drives; to sink wells, plant trees, build dams, erect housing; to combat the oppression of women and transform exploitative relations on the land; to free themselves from the imperialist yoke and solidarize with others engaged in that fight internationally. $24. Also in French.

WWW.PATHFINDERPRESS.COM

Strategic Victory
Along every road in the Sierra

Fidel Castro's firsthand account of 74 days of battle in the summer of 1958, when 300 revolutionary fighters—with the support of workers and peasants across Cuba—defeated the Batista dictatorship's 10,000-strong "encircle and annihilate offensive." Includes maps, photos, historical documents, illustrated glossary of weapons. 855 pp. In Spanish. $35

Strategic Counteroffensive
From the Sierra Maestra to Santiago de Cuba

Castro's day-by-day account of the final months of the revolutionary war in late 1958. How worker and peasant combatants, having defeated an army more than 30 times their size, launched a 147-day counteroffensive to extend the revolutionary struggle throughout Cuba, taking power January 1, 1959. Includes communiqués, letters, maps, and photos. 593 pp. In Spanish. $25
Published by Cuba's Council of State. $50 for two volume set.

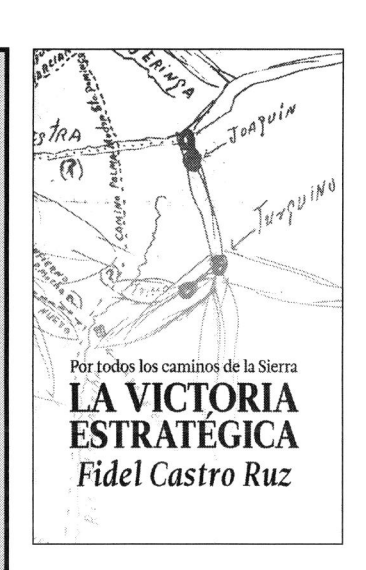

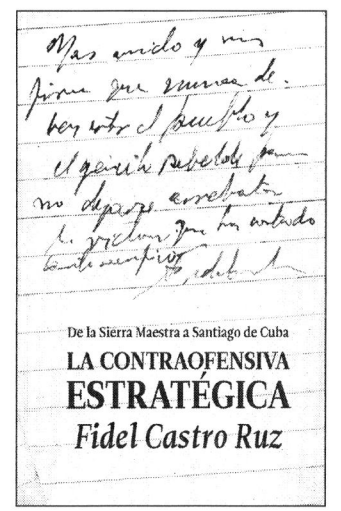

Che Guevara Talks to Young People

The Argentine-born revolutionary leader challenges youth of Cuba and the world to study, to work, to become disciplined. To join the front lines of struggles, small and large. To politicize themselves and the work of their organizations. To become a different kind of human being as they strive with working people of all lands to transform the world. Eight talks from 1959 to 1964. $15. Also in Spanish.

Socialism on Trial
JAMES P. CANNON

The basic ideas of socialism, explained in testimony during the 1941 trial of leaders of the Minneapolis Teamsters union and the Socialist Workers Party framed up and imprisoned under the notorious Smith "Gag" Act as the US rulers prepared to enter World War II. $16. Also in Spanish.

Capitalism's World Disorder
Working-Class Politics at the Millennium
JACK BARNES

The social devastation and financial panic, the coarsening of politics, the cop brutality and acts of imperialist aggression accelerating around us—all are the product not of something gone wrong with capitalism but of its lawful workings. Yet the future can be changed by the united struggle and selfless action of workers and farmers conscious of their power to transform the world. $25. Also in Spanish and French.

PATHFINDER AROUND THE WORLD

Visit our website for a complete list of titles and to place orders

www.pathfinderpress.com

PATHFINDER DISTRIBUTORS

UNITED STATES
(and Caribbean, Latin America, and East Asia)
Pathfinder Books, 306 W. 37th St., 10th Floor
New York, NY 10018

CANADA
Pathfinder Books, 7107 St. Denis, Suite 204
Montreal, QC H2S 2S5

UNITED KINGDOM
(and Europe, Africa, Middle East, and South Asia)
Pathfinder Books, First Floor, 120 Bethnal Green Road
(entrance in Brick Lane), London E2 6DG

AUSTRALIA
(and Southeast Asia and the Pacific)
Pathfinder, Level 1, 3/281-287 Beamish St., Campsie, NSW 2194
Postal address: P.O. Box 164, Campsie, NSW 2194

NEW ZEALAND
Pathfinder, 4/125 Grafton Road, Grafton, Auckland
Postal address: P.O. Box 3025, Auckland 1140

Join the Pathfinder Readers Club
to get 15% discounts on all Pathfinder titles
and bigger discounts on special offers.
Sign up at www.pathfinderpress.com
or through the distributors above.